How to be a Healthy & Happy Submissive

Kate Kinsey

ISBN: 1501093606
ISBN-13: 978-1501093609

In memory of
Shirley Beck

Chapter 1:
So you want to be a submissive....

Maybe you just read *that* book that everyone's been talking about. Or, if not *that* book, some other book. There are lots of them out there, especially now, even in the grocery store, right next to *Better Homes and Gardens*.

I'll admit it. I first felt the desire to be sexually dominated when I read *Gone with the Wind*. When Rhett grabbed Scarlett and carried her up those stairs — Phew! I wanted to experience that kind of passion and intensity.

But maybe for you, it was a movie about pirates or wild Scots in kilts kidnapping a damsel in distress, and you wanted to be that damsel with the heaving bosom in a virginal white night gown.

Maybe a partner once grabbed your hair and slapped your ass during sex, and you had the best orgasm *ever*. Now you're trying to figure out how to get him or her to do it again.

Maybe you stumbled onto an Internet porn site that shocked you — and made you wet at the same time.

There are a multitude of reasons you may have come looking for more information on dominance and submission. Let me set your mind at ease:

- There's nothing wrong with wanting a satisfying sex life.

- You have a RIGHT to a satisfying sex life.

- You are NOT the only person interested in "this kinky stuff." More people than you can imagine have been doing "this kinky stuff" for a long, long time.

- Feeling a need or desire to be dominated does not mean that you are weak, or broken, or not a "good feminist." *(More on that later.)*

Being turned on by being dominated, or wanting to serve someone in the most intimate ways, does not mean you have no self-esteem or no confidence in yourself.

It just means that something about this stuff makes your naughty bits all tingly, and that's perfectly okay.

What matters is how you pursue those desires. The purpose of this book is to give you the knowledge and tools to do it safely, sanely and consensually.

The first half of this book will explain the terminology and activities that make up the world of a submissive. The second half will give you specific advice on how to enter that world.

Disclaimer: I am giving you my personal opinions, based on years of my own experience. If you have looked around online at all, you've probably already found dozens of folks claiming they have the only answers, the "one true path" to complete and perfect submission.

Bullshit! If anyone — including me — tells you something that doesn't ring true to you, ignore it. If I suggest something that you can't use, throw it out. I don't mind, I promise.

Except, of course, for the single, cardinal, golden, never-to-broken rule that we will discuss in great detail in a later chapter: always be Safe, Sane and Consensual.

I am writing this for female submissives simply because those are the ones who keep finding me and asking how to begin this journey. Much of the same advice applies to male submissives as well, but there are many additional and specific challenges and issues, and frankly, I don't have that much experience with male submissives. If you are a male submissive reading this, please forgive me if the use of "her" and "she" makes you feel marginalized. It is certainly not my intent. At some point in the future, I will likely research and revise this book to apply more directly to the needs of the male submissive.

Kate Kinsey

Chapter 2:

What exactly is submission?

I chose the original title of this book — *How to Be a Submissive* — because it's the question I'm asked all the time: "How do I become a submissive?"

But I wasn't completely happy about that title because it implied that a submissive is something you can *become*. A submissive is something you *are*, not something you can learn to be. If there's not a spark of submission in your soul already, no amount of education, experience or "training" is going to make you a submissive. You might be able to fake it or to merely endure it, but you're going to hate every minute of it.

Does this mean you have to be a quiet, obedient good girl who always says yes? No. Does it mean you have to be dreaming of a life naked at the feet of a powerful master or mistress? No, of course not. Nor does it mean that you can't be a strong, independent individual with a mind of your own.

It simply means that some part of you is drawn to the idea of an intense physical and/or mental relationship where you surrender some degree of your personal power/will/control to another person whom you have chosen as worthy of that power.

Every person exists on a scale of dominance and submission. We all submit to parents, teachers, bosses and traffic cops, with varying degrees of success. When we *become* the parents, teachers, bosses and cops, we must embrace the dominant aspects of our personality.

So, no, you can't *become* a submissive. You can, however, choose to explore that part of your personality. If you have a strong enough leaning in that direction, you'll find that you will blossom and grow in ways you never dreamed were possible.

As I thought further about the title, I realized I didn't want to write a book about *just* being a submissive anyway. Being a submissive isn't really that hard; being a good submissive who is *happy* and *healthy* is the real trick.

An important message about fantasy and fiction:

You may have come to this book seeking the popular stereotype of dominance and submission found in bestsellers. Books and films are works of fiction, and they allow our imaginations to soar in ways that would never work in real life. The proliferation of such stories may lead you to believe that the only way to be a submissive is naked, on your knees, with a chain around your neck, learning seventy-eight ways to present yourself on the auction block to potential masters.

That is a fantasy, incorporating elements sometimes referred to as "high protocol," practiced by a very small number of people within the BDSM community.

If that's your fantasy, go for it. Most of us experience some elements of that on a very limited basis, but it's not the reality of submission in today's world.

In reality, submission is a very personal and fluid state that can be experienced in a hundred different ways:

- You may want to surrender all of your power, 24 hours a day, seven days a week (24-7); or you may want to only surrender a few hours on an erotic weekend.

- You may want to experience this kind of power exchange relationship only with a committed life partner, or you may want to experience casual, friendly fun with a variety of trusted partners, to varying degrees.

- You may only be interested in submitting sexually to your partner, while remaining an equal (or even dominant) partner outside the bedroom. Or you may yearn to have your dominant decide what clothes you wear, when you can speak and even when you can go to the bathroom.

- You may want to be "on top" one night with your partner, on the bottom the next. You may want to *always* be the dominant with one particular partner, and *always* be submissive with another.

- You may not be interested in sexual intercourse as a factor of your submission at all, but are seeking to enjoy the mental aspects of serving someone in a variety of ways.

- You may or may not be interested in experiencing

submission in the area of sadomasochism, through such activities as mild as a spanking or as intense as being whipped with a single-tail. Being submissive does NOT mean you have to be a masochist any more that being a dominant means someone has to be a sadist.

- You may be interested in being part of the larger kinky community, going to parties, conventions and other social/educational events; or you may only be interested in practicing submission with that one special person in the privacy of your own home.

There are as many different ways to be a submissive as there are submissives, and your preferences will change as you learn and grow. Your desires may also change depending upon the level of trust you have in your partner. Remember that this is all about the journey, not the destination.

There is no right or wrong way to "be" a submissive.
There is only the way that works for you and your partner,
as long as your relationship is safe, sane and consensual.

Chapter 3:
What does BDSM mean?

BDSM is what most people who practice dominance and submission call what we do. BDSM is a generic blanket term that encompasses a huge variety of lifestyles, fetishes, activities and kinks.

If you are going to explore your submission, you need to educate yourself about all the different ways people combine D/s (dominance and submission) with other components. (You may also see it referred to as M/s, for "master/slave.")

Think of a huge menu that includes every possible sexual expression you can think of (and many you never dreamed existed); this is the "buffet" we call BDSM. Each individual picks and chooses as many of these activities as appeal to them. Yes, there are some exotic-sounding dishes on this buffet, but not everybody tastes every dish, let alone makes it a part of their regular diet.

BDSM is generally accepted as an acronym for:

- **Bondage** – that is restraint of any kind; most common is rope bondage, but it can also include chains, cuffs, types of clothing like corsets and hoods.

- **Discipline** – the use of corporal punishment, often in conjunction with specific rules of behavior.

- The D in BDSM can also stand for **Dominance**, as in D/s dominance/submission, or power exchange, where one person has control consensually over another.

- **Sadomasochism** – the sexual enjoyment from either the infliction of, or experiencing of, pain and suffering, or some form of intense stimulation. The terms *sadist* and *masochist* have different connotations in BDSM than in the popular press or the psychology profession, and do not imply nonconsensual, uncaring, or undesirable behavior.

Generally, BDSM is defined as a sexual orientation or behavior among two or more adult partners that may include, but is not limited to, the use of physical and/or psychological stimulation to produce sexual arousal and satisfaction. Usually one partner will take an active role (top or dominant) and the other will take a passive role (bottom or submissive).

BDSM is a generic term; understand your personal kink(s).

Chapter 4: Pain? Really?

Do you have to like pain to be a submissive?

Short answer: no. Though many submissives do practice some form of sadomasochistic activity, like everything else, it is negotiable between you and whomever you decide to serve.

How can anyone *like* to experience pain?

Some people are just wired differently; for them, pain is directly erotic. Some people have orgasms from being flogged; others are highly aroused by nipple clamps. Keep in mind that pain is very subjective. What feels like pain to you may feel very different to me.

It's also about context. If you've ever experienced a hickey before, or found mysterious bruises the day after some strenuous sex, you already know how something that can feel like pain in one setting, can feel like pleasure when it's part of something else. That's why we say something "hurts so good."

Levels of stimulation

In many cases, the very term "pain" isn't really accurate. For many, BDSM activities (or "play") are about stimulation that can range from mild to intense. Much of our play focuses on exploring all the different sensations our flesh is capable of. We use absolutely anything and everything: feathers, ice cubes, guitar picks, needles, suction cups, warm (or hot) wax, fur, silk, teeth, electricity, Tiger Balm, rubber bands….

But yes, some people use pain in their play and it can be pretty intense. Sometimes, pain is used as means of testing obedience and endurance as the dominant enjoys an enormous sense of control. Sometimes, pain is merely a path to a natural high or altered consciousness that comes from the release of brain chemicals called endorphins.

Endorphins: brain candy

Endorphins are a group of morphine-like hormones secreted by the brain when the body is under unusual stress, which induce a sort of euphoria. Marathon runners and other athletes report the same feeling when they have pushed their bodies to the very edge of their endurance. It's an incredible and entirely natural high. Some people refer to it as *subspace,* though others believe subspace is something completely separate. We'll talk more about that later.

People throughout history, in many religions all over the world, have used pain as a means to reach another level of consciousness or to prove their faith. Catholic saints flogged themselves, Native Americans underwent extreme tests of manhood, and Hindus walked on hot coals. Utilizing pain is nothing new.

**It's not just about pain;
it's about experiencing all the glorious
sensations of which our bodies are capable.**

Kate Kinsey

Chapter 5:

Your BDSM may not be my BDSM

Because BDSM encompasses so many different interests and fetishes, it can be a very confusing term. You may meet someone who says they are into BDSM, and you're thinking, "Oh goody! I can ask him to tie me up!'

And then it turns out he's not into bondage at all. When he said he was "into" BDSM, he meant he was into D/s (dominance and submission). He only wants you to wear high heels to the grocery store and call him "sir." This is why it is so important to understand all these terms, and to communicate clearly with any potential partner.

What confuses some people is that all these activities often overlap. BUT THEY DON'T HAVE TO, and they don't for everyone.

- You can enjoy being tied up and not be a submissive.
- You can be a submissive and not enjoy being tied up.
- You can enjoy applying discipline and not be a sadist.
- You can enjoy dominance and submission, and not be into *any* of these physical activities like flogging, bondage or discipline.

Think back to the analogy of a sexual menu. No one eats everything on a buffet. You know at once that some things appeal to you, like fried chicken or chocolate cake. But perhaps other things look interesting, too, and if you are adventurous, you put just a little on your plate to see if you like it.

If you do like it, you go back for more. If you don't, you are allowed to spit it out, and leave the rest on your plate. (Just remember that you aren't allowed to point at someone else's plate and go, "Eeeewww, how can you even think about eating that?" That's just rude.)

If you look at a buffet in any restaurant, you'd be hard pressed to find two people with exactly the same thing on their plates, in the same proportion.

No one is going to tell you what you have to eat at the BDSM buffet. They may say, "You should try the sushi, it's fabulous!" but you are allowed to say, "No, thanks."

Nor should they tell you that you can't create something entirely new from the buffet items. If you want to stir jambalaya into your mashed potatoes and pour Ranch dressing over it, go for it, if that's what your taste buds are craving.

Take what you want, and leave the rest.

Chapter 6:
What BDSM is not

BDSM is **not** a mental illness. The American Psychiatric Association's states that SM (sadomasochism) only becomes a diagnosable dysfunction when:

> *"the fantasies, sexual urges, or behaviors cause clinically significant distress or impairment in social, occupational or other important areas of functioning."*

Healthy BDSM is when two or more adults consent to exchange energy, power, sensations or experiences (however mild or extreme) in ways that fuel their mutual happiness and fulfillment. Both parties are actively invested in the well-being of each other and themselves.

- BDSM is NOT about abuse or violence.
- BDSM is voluntary.
- BDSM is consensual.
- BDSM partners are informed.
- BDSM partners ask for and enjoy the behavior.
- BDSM partners take care to make their activities as safe as possible.

For some, BDSM is a way to spice up their relationships; it may never extend outside the bedroom. For others it is a way of living life, and you'll hear these people describe themselves as "24-7" or "lifestyle."

Neither is right or wrong, better or worse, though unfortunately you may run into someone who will try to tell you that their way is the only right way. All of us came into this lifestyle to express what we really are, to satisfy needs and desires that are an intrinsic part of us. It's foolish to come into the BDSM community assuming that one-size-fits all when we know it didn't work that way in the vanilla world.

BDSM is not about violence or abuse, but a mutually satisfying relationship emphasizing consent, communication, honesty and care for your partner.

Chapter 7: Power Exchange

"Power exchange" is specifically the dominance/submission (D/s) area of BDSM. It refers more to the psychological components of BDSM (as opposed to the physical components) when the partners agree to an exchange of power, ownership, command, or property rights. The submissive consensually transfers their power to the dominant. The power actually goes both ways because the dominant, by controlling and caring for the submissive, actually empowers the submissive to be who and what they truly are.

The degree to which someone gives over or accepts power over another is a matter of personal choice. There is no rule that says if you are a submissive, you MUST do this. You and your partner work out what feels right to you both.

Some people who practice D/s don't feel it has anything to do with the other activities like bondage or spanking. I've heard one D/s practitioner say that he lives a D/s lifestyle, and all the rest of it is just "kinky sex." Conversely, some people believe they can practice bondage and SM without any kind of power exchange at all.

There is another school of thought that believes that *every* BDSM relationship, whether casual or long-term, involves an exchange of power. The only difference is that some power exchanges are situational and very limited; it may only last thirty minutes during a play scene at a dungeon party, while others affect every part of someone's life, all the time. Many more people fall somewhere in between the two extremes.

The brain is the largest erogenous zone. Use it.

Chapter 8: Dominance

Dominance is a personality trait someone exhibits. *Dominants* are generally confident people who like to be in charge. They are "natural" leaders and problem solvers. A dominant accepts responsibility as well as authority, and is in control of their own life and their emotions.

This is not to be confused with "domineering." Think about the difference between a good leader and a bully:

A good dominant listens to what others have to say; a domineering bully rarely does.

When a good dominant disagrees with someone, he or she will discuss their point of view calmly and respectfully.

A bully will simply shout other people down.

A good dominant takes responsibility for his or her mistakes; a bully always blames someone else.

A good dominant cares about the well being of what belongs to him; a bully only cares about getting what he or she wants.

A good dominant is always honest. A bully uses half-truths and omission to spin the situation to his advantage.

Many dominants are sadists; many are not. Many dominants feel a very compelling need to care for and protect their submissive(s). The degree to which a dominant exercises control over their submissive is a matter of personal choice. Some dominants choose to micromanage the smallest details of their sub's life, down to what they eat and what they wear. Others set general guidelines and leave it to the submissive to figure out the best way to fulfill them.

Being a dominant in a D/s relationship is most definitely not about getting their way all the time. There are enormous responsibilities that go along with the role.

A dominant may be male or female. Generally, a female dominant is referred to as a domme, spelled differently but pronounced the same way as "dom," though some people will say "dom-MAY." An important distinction is that a female dominant is NOT a dominatrix, which usually refers to a professional who provides the service of domination for payment.

Many dominants feel that this is "who they *are*," whereas being a "top" or "topping" is what they – or other people -- *do*.

Some dominants don't feel they "choose" to be dominant or to take a dominant role; it is simply what comes naturally to them. Some feel that you cannot learn to be a dominant.

Some believe that most of us have some dominant traits and some submissive traits. And the beauty of BDSM is that you can choose which aspect of your personality you want to explore. This is where the term "switch" comes in.

Chapter 9:
Switches, tops and bottoms

A **switch** is someone who enjoys both roles: sometimes they are dominant, and sometimes they are submissive. Some are always dominant with a specific partner but submissive to someone else. Some switches are completely at ease with taking either role with anybody; they can even change roles mid-scene.

A lot of people will use the terms *top* and *dominant* interchangeably, as well as *bottom* and *submissive*. This gets confusing because these terms apply to two distinct types of personalities and behaviors that need to be defined. The activities they engage in may be the same, but the motivation for doing it is quite different.

We use the term *bottom* and *top* when we are referring to kinky play in which a power exchange, if it's present at all, is a minor element. The major focus is on the activity going on.

A *top* is a role one assumes. Topping is taking the active role in a scene, usually giving sensation or pain, or controlling the scene. But whereas most dominants feel that they are *always* dominant, topping is generally considered to end when the scene ends. Again, it's an activity, not a state of being.

A dominant may be a top, but a top does not have to be a dominant. I have known tops that like to be dominant within a scene while they play with someone, but have absolutely no interest in dominating anyone or anything once the play is done.

Likewise, many submissives also top. I am primarily submissive, but I can and do top sometimes, though never my master. But I have known other slaves and submissives that have been trained to top their masters or mistresses.

How is this possible? Because some dominants may also be masochists or they may simply enjoy the pleasures of "bottoming" — having certain things done to them — though they retain their dominance by giving all directions of exactly what should be done and how. Those submissives trained to top their masters or mistresses do so precisely because it gives their dominant pleasure, and are often referred to as *service tops.*

The idea that you can choose which aspect of your personality to explore also explains those people whose BDSM life is the exact opposite of their day-to-day vanilla life. It is very common to find people in high-powered authority positions (doctors, lawyers, corporate CEOs) who choose to be submissive in their BDSM life because they need that release; it excites them to let go of that control.

I consider myself a submissive because I have a need and desire to be dominated and/or controlled. Dominant men (and some women) excite me, and all my life, I've had a tendency to want to obey and/or please dominant personalities. When I came into this lifestyle, I thought I was only interested in sexual domination, meaning that I wanted it in the bedroom only; I thought that if someone tried it anywhere else, I'd laugh in his face.

But I learned to never say never. When I found the right dominant for me, I suddenly found myself wanting to do all kinds of things for him, including iron his shirts and fetch him another glass of wine. The right dominant will do that: he will inspire you to submit.

I am not submissive to everyone. I am submissive to those who fit my personal definition of a dominant. (In fact, many who meet me for the first time are surprised to learn I am a submissive; I suspect this is a nice way of saying I'm a little bitchy.) You have to trust and respect someone before submitting to him or her, whether short term in play (within a scene) or in a relationship.

The difference between bottoming and submitting

There are times when I play that I am merely *bottoming*, not submitting in any real way. There is no serious power exchange. Sometime I want a good flogging, and I'm in it purely for the stress release and the endorphin rush. I don't really feel any pressing need to please the person topping me. When it stops being fun for me, I use my safe word and the play is over. *That* is bottoming.

Submitting, on the other hand, is when your primary motivation is to please the person to whom you have given even a temporary and limited control over you. You will do things you don't enjoy – sometimes things you even fear and loathe – because the need to please and obey the dominant is that compelling, and because doing so gives you pleasure or satisfaction. Many submissives find pleasure and satisfaction in giving service of a completely non-sexual nature.

That is not to say that if you are submissive, you have no rights or that you never say no. A submissive is not a doormat. Doormats are not fun to dominate. Most submissives I know are strong, capable individuals. They have to be.

**You can't give your personal power to a dominant
if you don't have any power to begin with.**

Chapter 10:
Are you a submissive or a bottom?

The distinction between bottoming and submitting is important because many people come to the kinky community believing they are a submissive because they want to be tied up, or they like to be spanked.

So they try to do all the things a good submissive is supposed to do, and find that they hate it. They aren't comfortable surrendering any part of their personal power and don't enjoy someone else taking control of them.

That's because they are bottoms, not submissives. There is nothing at all wrong with that. You can have a lot of fun as a bottom. Tops, sadists and even dominants enjoy playing with bottoms, especially if they happen to be masochists. Everybody just has to be clear about what they are hoping to get out of a relationship or a play session.

I remember the first time I saw my master play with a bottom, I didn't understand the difference, and I was absolutely horrified by the way she interacted with him. She resisted, she taunted, she had all kinds of demands about how she should be restrained, and, at one point, she even *spit her gum at him!* I watched from a corner of the dungeon, literally squirming and wincing, getting angry with this terrible submissive for being so disrespectful to him. I didn't understand why he allowed her to get away with that kind of behavior; he even laughed about it!

Afterward, he explained that she was not a submissive at all, but a bottom. She was there to have a good time, and that was it. Going into the play knowing that, he was not expecting her submission, nor forcing his dominance on her. She was interested in his considerable abilities as a top. He was interested in the things he could do with her. *Then* I got it.

There's nothing wrong with being a bottom, as long as you and your partners understand what that means.

Chapter 11:
The difference between a
dominant and a master

Many people use the terms *dominant* and *master* interchangeably. It's better to understand the distinctions between them as you navigate through the kinky world.

Technically, a dominant does not have to be a master or mistress. Some dominants don't even *want* to be a master or mistress because of the added responsibility it brings. To be a master or mistress implies that someone is the master of *someone else*, either a slave or submissive.

Think of it as the difference between being a renter or a homeowner. Most good renters will try to take reasonable care of their homes, but a homeowner is far more invested in it. *All* the care of that property falls to the homeowner; there's no landlord to call when the roof leaks. It's an enormous responsibility not to be taken lightly.

Generally, "Master" or "Mistress" is a title used only in a negotiated relationship. No one will ever become your master or mistress without your specific consent.

There is no worldwide BDSM board of standards that decides

who is qualified to be a master or mistress. It's an unfortunate fact that anybody who can type can get on the Internet and call himself "Lord Master High Mucky-Mucky of the House of Pretentious Wannabes." With very few exceptions, those kinds of titles mean absolutely nothing.

There are those who have chosen to include Master or Mistress or Lord or Emperor or whatever in their "scene names" — those pseudonyms many use to protect their privacy — and the rest of the community is a good sport about it. In those cases, it is a name, not any kind of earned title. In those cases, it is good manners to address someone as "Master Smith" but you wouldn't call him *your* "master."

No one has the right to insist you address him or her as such unless you are in a negotiated relationship with him or her. Generally, we all use the rules of common courtesy when we socialize. "Sir" and "ma'am" are simply respectful ways to address anyone.

Remember: whether you are a dominant or a submissive – **you are not dominant or submissive to every person in the world,** and other people generally don't take it well when you assume that you are or that they are.

**You don't always have to be submissive,
but you should always be polite.**

Chapter 12:
Old Guard and High Protocol

Old Guard refers to the roots of modern BDSM in the exclusively gay male SM leather culture that rose up after WWII. Old Guard members took a highly regimented, quasi-militaristic approach to power exchange and SM. Think of the stereotypical old-fashioned gay "leather man" clad in black leather from head to toe with lots of studs, chains and straps. That's Old Guard.

In the Old Guard, no one could become a master until they had served as a submissive. That is how they trained new masters. Very few people — either gay or heterosexual — do this anymore. When someone says they are Old Guard or *Old School,* they generally mean that they started on the bottom and worked their way up.

Or they may be making stuff up to impress you and everybody else. It's hard to tell sometimes. Someone who is authentically Old Guard would be both gay and nearly ninety years old by now. There are those in the leather community who dismiss the whole myth of the Old Guard as silly nonsense. But someone who identifies himself as Old Guard is generally someone who practices BDSM with a high degree of protocol.

Protocol is a very specific set of rules for conduct and procedures in a certain setting. High protocol practitioners of BDSM are generally what you see in erotic fiction, but they do exist in real life. Slaves are naked or dressed in a manner dictated by their masters; they have very strict rules for when and how they may speak, eat and even sleep. It is a highly ritualized lifestyle that appeals to those dominants and submissives desiring an extreme degree of control and submission.

Obviously, some protocol is higher than others. Every master and slave has to find a balance that is practical in day-to-day life. Family and finances have a huge impact on whether someone can make a high protocol BDSM relationship work. Some are able to live within that construct simply because these relationships can, from the outside, appear very much like a traditional 1950s marriage. Some have to compromise by restricting their protocol to behind closed doors.

Many BDSM couples will indulge in a little high protocol from time to time, even if they don't try to live it 24/7. They may have certain rituals for when they go out to the local dungeon club, or for evenings when they have time alone. Some consider it merely role-playing as part of the fantasy; for others, it is an important reflection of who and what they are.

**Respect the choices of others,
and insist that they respect yours.**

Chapter 13: 24/7

Another term you'll hear is "24/7," as in, "twenty-four hours a day, seven days a week." Some people will say they "live" a BDSM lifestyle 24/7, but as with anything else, you have to ask exactly what that means to them.

Some say they live it 24/7 and they mean they do it with strict protocol. Some simply mean that everything they do is a reflection of their D/s relationship, all the time.

A 24/7 high protocol style of BDSM is exceptionally difficult to accomplish. It takes a particular personality (beyond merely dominant and submissive) on both sides to even attempt it. It requires enormous self control to put aside the way you've lived all your life and inhabit the role of either dominant or submissive not just for a few hours, or even a few days, but around the clock within strict parameters.

Some try it and find it's simply too exhausting. Even some of the best dominants and masters just don't want to be dominant at 4:30 in the morning.

I only have issues with those who live as Master/slave 24/7 when they have a kinkier-than-thou attitude that they "really live it" while the rest of us are just "playing at it."

To make it work, you have to be adept at juggling, and slipping in and out of role, because there are areas where you simply can't bring your kink as fully as you might like. Consider doctors' visits and legal issues like mortgages, business, childcare, jobs, etc.

Sure, if you have enough wealth that allows you to keep your slave(s) at home, and a career/family that allows you to be openly kinky, you can do a lot more with less interference. But most of us don't have that luxury.

More often, people will aim for a high level of dominance and submissive 24/7, and eventually find a compromise that works for them. That's all that matters, really.

24/7 is not a "higher" form of BDSM.

Chapter 14:
Ceremonies, titles and contracts

Some have constructed elaborate rituals for "capping" (presenting someone with a leather hat) or some other ceremony to bestow master status on someone. Rituals can be fun and they can play an important part of celebrating someone's personal journey, but don't let anybody tell you that their ritual is (or should be) central to someone *else's* journey. There is no official or historically honored ritual that everyone practices, any more than there is an official authority to decide who is and is not a master or slave.

There are those who have constructed websites and registries for slaves, and they can be exciting — just like those "official" contracts some people will try to sell you — but it's just window-dressing for the fantasy. The rituals, titles, registries, and contracts don't have any real meaning or value except *what an individual chooses to give them*.

Does that mean they aren't important? No, I wouldn't say that, either.

When you get right down to it, practically everything we do in BDSM is about living out our fantasies, about taking what is inside us and letting it shine on the outside, too. We use a lot of props and costumes, from collars to handcuffs to leather outfits.

We play with a lot of toys, some of which are pretty intricate, and we construct elaborate scenes complete with mood music.

Weddings, graduations, christenings and funerals are just a few examples of how we use rituals in the vanilla world to show how important something is to us, for celebrating rites of passage and dealing with powerful emotions. If using a ritual or ceremony in your BDSM life enhances your pleasure or relationship, then by all means, do it!

If a contract with your dominant helps you both understand what you hope to get out of the relationship and what responsibilities you have to each other, that's a very useful thing. It doesn't hurt that it can also be a big turn-on. Just remember that it's no more legally binding than a grocery list.

If having your master register you as a slave on some website helps you both find the headspace you're craving, do it. Have a certificate printed up and frame it on the wall above your bed!

Just remember that it may mean nothing at all to anyone else, and that you have no right to require anyone else to do it. Neither does anyone else have the right to require you to do it if you don't want to.

**Rituals, contracts and titles can be useful and fun,
but they are not required.**

40

Chapter 15:
Collars and their meaning

Collars are one of the most sacred symbols in the kink community, and also one of the most abused. For a submissive, the collar is the symbol of everything she yearns for. It's not just physical proof that she belongs to someone to whom she has surrendered, but also proof of her dominant's love and protection. The collar shows the world (or as much of it as is practical) that someone has claimed her as *his*.

Most people view the collar as the D/s equivalent of a wedding band. It is a symbol, not only of ownership and submission, but the commitment of both partners. One gives, one takes and together they complete the circle of the power exchange.

It's been a mixed blessing that our modern culture has co-opted the collar as a fashion statement. On the one hand, there are teenagers running around in studded collars that don't know and don't care that it may have any meaning at all beyond that of trendy jewelry.

On the other hand, the more common sighting of collars everywhere makes it less likely to draw negative attention when we stop to pump gas on the way to a party. It has also given us more styles of collars to choose from than ever before. You can still buy your collar at the local pet shop, but you don't have to stand there trying them on between the forty-pound bags of kibble and the cat litter, unless of course, that's your master's idea of fun.

Most submissives do not wear their collar everyday, unless it is one chosen specifically to pass as "ordinary" jewelry. Some only wear the collar among other members of the community. These days, almost anything can be used as collar; the style is not as important as the meaning behind it. They may lock, or they may not. If a lock is used, the dominant generally retains the key.

Play, consideration, protection and training collars

Some people — but by no means all — use different types of collars for different types of relationships, or different stages within a relationship. Some dominants and even tops will ask a submissive to wear a *play collar* during a scene or session as a prop to put the submissive in the proper headspace, or simply as a place to attach a leash or chain. At the end of the play, the collar comes off and is put away.

There is a *collar of consideration* — which means exactly what it says, that the wearer is being considered by a dominant. You could consider it a "dating" collar, and either party can take it off at any time.

A collar of protection is sometimes given to a submissive simply to tell the rest of the world that someone is looking out for her. Often this occurs with very new submissives, or those getting over an abusive relationship or some other personal issue that makes them particularly vulnerable. A submissive wearing a collar of protection is not to be approached except through the protecting dominant. The protecting dominant should ideally be someone respected by his peers who will not use his position to take advantage of the submissive.

Then there is the *training collar,* which some view as the equivalent of an engagement ring. However, those who subscribe to the notion of "training" submissives with whom they have no emotional relationship, would view it as a much more impersonal symbol of that status.

The *final* or *formal collar,* symbolizing serious commitment from both parties, is often (but not always) presented during a collaring ceremony. The ritual may be as elaborate as a wedding, or simply a gathering of special friends to witness the event.

There are different opinions as to when, where and how such a collar may be removed. Just as some reject the possibility of divorce, so, too, some D/s practitioners believe that the collar can only be removed under the most serious and grave circumstances. Some believe that only the dominant can remove a collar.

But let's be honest: a collar is a strip of leather or metal, and it can be taken off at any time. There is nothing legally binding about a collar. Nothing at all prevents a submissive from taking off the collar and walking away.

Legal considerations

The flip side is that neither party has any legal rights if their union isn't in conjunction with a marriage license. This is an important thing to consider if you enter into a long-term commitment with someone that, for whatever reason, you cannot or will not marry. You and your partner need to consult a lawyer about powers of attorney and other such tools to be used in case of emergencies.

Easy on, easy off

You may hear another term used: *Velcro collar*. It means what it sounds like: a collar easily put on and taken off. Generally people use the term as an insult, often referring to people who style themselves as kinksters but don't really (according to the speaker) understand or respect the nuances of the community.

While you may be tempted to wear some kind of collar as a fashion accessory, or to "feel" more like a submissive, don't. It's considered bad taste.

A collar is only as meaningful
as the relationship it represents.

Chapter 16: Finding your limits

When you first venture out to play, potential partners will ask, "What are your limits?" It's perfectly okay to tell someone that you are still learning what your limits are.

Below is a list of activities taken from a commonly used negotiation checklist. Often, dominants will give a potential play partner this sort of list and ask them to rate each activity as one of the following:

1. You don't want to do or like to do this activity, but wouldn't object if it were asked of you.
2. You are willing to do this activity, but it has no special appeal for you.
3. You usually like doing this activity, at least on an irregular/occasional basis.
4. You like doing this activity, and would like to experience it on a regular basis.
5. The activity is a wild turn-on for you, and you would like it as often as possible.
6. You've never done this activity before and don't really know how you feel about.

A Common Negotiation Checklist

Abrasion:	Age play:
Anal sex:	Anal plugs (small):
Anal plugs (large):	Anal plug (public, under clothes):
Animal roles:	Arm & leg sleeves (arm binders):
Asphyxiation:	Auctioned for charity:
Bathroom use control:	Bestiality:
Beating (soft):	Bisexual Activity with Another Sub:
Blindfolds:	Being serviced (sexually):
Being bitten:	Breast/chest bondage:
Breath control:	Branding:
Boot worship:	Bondage (light):
Bondage (heavy):	Bondage (multi-day):
Bondage (public, under clothing):	Breast whipping:
Brown showers (scat):	Cages (locked inside of):
Caning:	Catheterization:
Cells/Closets (locked inside of):	Chastity belts:
Chauffeuring:	Choking:
Clothespins:	Cock worship:
Collars (worn in private):	Collars (worn in public):
Competitions (with other Subs):	Corsets (wearing):
Cuffs (leather):	Cuffs (metal):

Cutting:	Dilation:
Double penetration:	Electricity:
Enemas:	Enforced chastity:
Examinations (physical):	Exercise (forced/required):
Exhibitionism (friends):	Exhibitionism (strangers):
Eye contact restrictions:	Face slapping:
Fantasy abandonment:	Fantasy rape:
Fantasy gang-rape:	Fisting (anal):
Fisting (vaginal):	Following orders:
Foot worship:	Forced dressing:
Forced homosexuality:	Forced masturbation:
Forced nudity (private):	Forced nudity (around others):
Forced servitude:	Full head hoods:
Gags (cloth):	Gags (rubber):
Gags (tape):	Gates of Hell (male):
Genital sex:	Given away to another Dom (temp):
Given away to another Dom (perm):	Golden showers:
Hairbrush spankings:	Hair pulling:
Hand jobs (giving):	Hand jobs (receiving):
Harems (serving w/other subs):	Harnessing (leather):
Harnessing (rope):	Having food chosen for you:
Having clothing chosen for you:	Head (giving fellatio):

Head (receiving fellatio):	High heel worship:
Homage with tongue (non-sexual):	Hot oils (on genitals):
Hot waxing:	Housework (doing):
Human puppy dog:	Humiliation (private):
Humiliation (public):	Hypnotism:
Ice cubes:	Infantilism:
Initiation rites:	Injections:
Intricate (Japanese) rope bondage:	Interrogations:
Kidnapping:	Kneeling:
Leather clothing:	Leather restraints:
Lectures for misbehavior:	Licking (non-sexual):
Manacles & Irons:	Manicures (giving):
Massage (giving):	Massage (receiving):
Medical scenes:	Modeling for erotic photos:
Mouth bits:	Mummification:
Nipple clamps:	Nipple weights:
Oral/anal play (rimming):	Over-the-knee spanking:
Orgasm denial:	Orgasm control:
Outdoor scenes:	Outdoor sex:
Phone sex (serving Dom):	Phone sex (serving Dom's friends):
Piercing (temporary, play-pierce):	Piercing (permanent):
Prison scenes:	Pony slave:
Public exposure:	Pussy/cock whipping:

Pussy worship:	Riding crops:
Riding the "horse" (crotch tort.):	Rituals:
Religious scenes:	Restrictive rules on behavior:
Rubber/latex clothing:	Rope body harness:
Saran wrapping:	Scratching - getting:
Scratching - giving:	Sensory deprivation:
Serving:	Serving as art:
Serving as ashtray:	Serving as furniture:
Serving as a maid:	Serving as toilet:
Serving as waitress/waiter:	Serving orally (sexual):
Serving other doms (supervised):	Serving other doms (unsupervised):
Sexual deprivation (short term):	Sexual deprivation (long term):
Shaving (body hair):	Shaving (head hair):
Sleep deprivation:	Sleepsacks:
Slutty clothing (private):	Slutty clothing (public):
Spanking:	Spandex clothing:
Speech restrictions (when, what):	Speculums (Anal):
Speculums (vaginal):	Spreader bars:
Standing in corner:	Stocks:
Straight jackets:	Strap-on-dildos (sucking on):
Strap-on-dildos (penetrated by):	Strap-on-dildos (wearing):
Strapping (full body beating):	Suspension (upright):

Suspension (inverted):	Suspension (horizontal):
Supplying new partners for Dom:	Swallowing semen:
Swallowing urine:	Swapping (with one other couple):
Swinging (multiple couples):	Tattooing:
Teasing:	Tickling:
Triple penetration:	Uniforms:
Including others:	Vaginal dildo:
Verbal humiliation:	Vibrator on genitals:
Voyeurism (watching others):	Voyeurism (your Dom w/others)
Video (watching others):	Video (recordings of you):
Water torture:	Wearing symbolic jewelry:
Whipping:	Wooden paddles:
Wrestling:	

Don't panic if you don't know what some of these things are; most are not as scary as they sound and you certainly won't be asked to do all of them right away. Some of them, you may *never* be asked to do, and you never have to.

Depending on where, when, how and with whom you begin to play, you may never even see a list like this. Sometimes the negotiation is just a conversation. But when you see just how many different activities commonly occur in BDSM play, you understand the importance of learning how to ask for what you want, and how to tell someone what you don't want. Those things make up your personal "limits." If you don't know what something is, ask!

LIMITS: boundaries of consent as negotiated between partners. Negotiation is when you talk about what you would love to do, what you might consider doing, and then what you absolutely refuse to do. Limits can be anything you want them to be, and everybody has limits, even if the limits are as wide open as "no death or dismemberment."

Newbie Mistake to Avoid:

Many new submissives are so eager to play that they will say "Oh, I have no limits; you can do whatever you like!"

Now, I understand what they mean when they say this, because I was one of the newbies who used to say it. What I *really* meant was that I wanted to experience everything and anything (almost), and that I was fairly sure these people I knew and trusted weren't going to suggest anything too dangerous or outrageous (and I really did have pretty liberal limits). I was always an overachiever, so I also wanted to prove just how good a submissive and bottom I was.

But I quickly learned just what a stupid thing it was to say when someone said, "Okay, I want to shave your head."

Don't say you have "no limits." It just makes you look naïve and could lead to something totally unexpected.

The most common limits include: no drawing blood; no permanent damage; no genital contact or penetration; no scat; no golden showers; no children; no animals. One limit you seriously need to consider is whether or not bruising is acceptable. Some people have to be careful that bruises, hickeys and bite marks don't show.

Dominants and tops have limits, too; don't take it personally if you want to do something and your play partner declines.

- **Hard limits:** the maximum edge of someone's negotiated limit. In some cases, a hard limit is a personal choice; I personally cannot tolerate being tickled. In other cases, it's a health or safety issue. For example, if the submissive is allergic to latex, any latex product is a "hard limit."

- **Soft limits**: things you really aren't wild about doing. I personally don't care much for paddles, and I will tell a top, "If you really want to use a paddle, I'll try to take as much as I can, but if you decide to skip the paddle, I'll be perfectly happy." Of course, I learned too late that saying such a thing to a sadist is not a good idea, because that is exactly what he or she will do to you.

- **Pushing limits:** Some submissives agree to let the dominant push him or her to a limit and slightly beyond. Most commonly this occurs when the submissive believes her limits stem from an irrational fear that she hopes the dominant will help her to overcome.

- **Respecting limits:** A fundamental ethic among kinky people is to treat limits as a sacred trust, and never to violate the submissive's trust by non-consensually exceeding their limits.

- Your limits will change as you gain experience.

- You are not required to explain or justify your limits!

For a top/dominant to intentionally violate a bottom's stated limits or boundaries is nonconsensual and unethical. Someone who does that is shunned by their local community, and the word spreads until no one is willing to play with them. In many cases, a person can be banned from organizations and events. We take limits that seriously. We'll talk more about the issue of consent in a later chapter.

This is why negotiation is so vital. When you think of how many different activities that can fall under the heading of BDSM, then you realize why you have to negotiate in a fairly detailed way.

**Learn your personal limits
and insist that they be respected.**

Kate Kinsey

Chapter 17: Negotiation

You should negotiate everything, but we'll talk specifically about negotiating a relationship or a specific scene.

- **Negotiating a relationship:** communication aimed at reaching a clear, consensual agreement with your partner about the type of relationship you will have and the kinds of things you will do together. The negotiation process lasts as long as needed to hammer these things out: it can be days, weeks, months or years. Couples may also re-negotiate periodically as their relationship evolves and their needs change.

- **Negotiating a scene** involves a much narrower type of dialogue, in which partners only decide on what they will do during a scene. Negotiating a scene does not have to be stiff and formal. It can occur within the flirtatious conversations of getting to know one another. But it definitely needs to happen before any kind of play commences.

Ultimately, everybody wants to have a good time. Negotiation is about making sure that happens. Nobody goes into a scene thinking, "I really want to ruin someone's night."

We negotiate for safety reasons as well. You want to inform your partner of any physical problems you may have, be it diabetes or bad knees. But you also do it so that you or your partner doesn't end up having a really bad or unpleasant experience.

It would be so much nicer if we weren't afraid to negotiate when we first started having sex! We so often are afraid of hurting someone's feelings or making a fool of ourselves, that we just lie there and just hope that our partner will do what we want them to. That almost never works, and we end up having a lot of mediocre sex.

So don't be afraid to negotiate! Talk about what you enjoy and what you don't. Get as detailed as you possibly can.

> *Hint: If you feel awkward using explicit language to talk about your desires, find a friend to practice with. I highly recommend new submissives find another submissive (not a dominant) with whom they can work on issues like these. Even saying such things aloud to yourself in the shower will help you loosen up and feel more comfortable.*
>
> *If you absolutely cannot say certain things out loud, then write it out! Just make sure you can communicate your wants and desires.*

Chapter 18:
Safe, Sane and Consensual

There is only one ironclad rule in BDSM: whatever we do should be **safe, sane, and consensual** (or **SSC**).

But what does that mean, really? Your idea of "safe" and "sane," and my idea of "safe" and "sane" may not be the same; they may not even be in the same neighborhood. I don't think motorcycles are safe or sane, but people ride them everyday.

Just like driving a car, there are risks in every single BDSM activity. Nothing we do is 100% risk-free, and it's dangerous to kid ourselves that it is. Bondage is one of the most common types of play that people engage in, but it can also be the single most dangerous. (This is because bondage seems so simple and safe that people frequently get careless, and that's when accidents happen.)

So what do we mean by safe?

Go back to the car analogy. Thousands of people die each year in traffic accidents, but we don't stop driving. Instead, we pass laws that you have to be a certain age to be trusted with operating a car.

Then you have to take a driver's education class, and two different tests (learner's and regular) before you get a license. We learn the laws and traffic signals. We wear a seat belt, we keep our car in good working condition, and we don't drive when we are impaired. If we do all that, then we have made driving as safe as we possibly can.

It's the same with BDSM play. By safe, we don't mean without risk. We mean we take no risks that can easily be avoided. We find out as much as we can about safe techniques and safety concerns associated with any given activity. We engage in those activities prepared for things that can go wrong.

For example, if you are into bondage, one of the best things you can do for your safety or that of your partner is to get a pair of EMT scissors and keep them nearby whenever you play, so that if something goes wrong — someone gets dizzy, pulls a muscle, has a seizure or the house catches on fire — you can release them quickly.

Safety includes the responsibility of protecting yourself and your partner from STD (sexually transmitted disease) infection including the HIV virus.

So what about sane?

Sane is knowing the difference between fantasy and reality. Most of these bestselling books and kinky sites on the Internet are distorted for fantasy's sake, and are not representative of real situations and relationships. Sane is knowing that just because you saw something online or read it in a book, you shouldn't necessarily try it yourself.

Sane is knowing that *real* slavery is something you wouldn't enjoy, and that you're seeking to act out a fantasy from which you can escape at any time.

But there's another aspect of differentiating between fantasy and reality, and that is the false belief that bad things and accidents happen to other people, not to you.

The reality is that accidents and bad things can happen to anybody at any time. If you agree to meet someone from the Internet for the first time in private because you think nothing bad will ever happen to you, you're not grounded in reality. If you think you can get away with having unprotected sex because HIV or some other sexually transmitted disease won't happen to you, you're not living in reality. Part of *sane* is accepting responsibility for your actions and knowing that there are consequences.

Sane also distinguishes between mental illness and health. A real distinction between mental illness and health is when a behavior pattern causes problems in a person's life. Washing your hands until the skin is peeling off, or so frequently that you cannot otherwise function is a sign of mental illness. Is it a mental illness to enjoy BDSM activities? No, but it may be if you're so consumed by the practice of it that you can't hold a job or pay your bills.

What is consensual?

Consensual is respecting the limits imposed by each participant at all times.

Consent is the prime ingredient of BDSM. Without free and complete consent, sex becomes rape. Without consent, a spanking or flogging scene becomes criminal assault.

Informed consent means that a person agrees to do something or have something done to them in full understanding of the activity. This is why all forms of pedophilia, bestiality and necrophilia are unethical as well as illegal: children, animals and corpses cannot give consent. Sex with the mentally handicapped or someone who is drunk or stoned is also unethical because they do not have a complete understand of what they are consenting to.

Dominants and submissives are equally responsible for making sure they are safe, sane and consensual.

Chapter 19: Safe words

One of the most common tools of communication within a scene is called a **safe word.** A safe word is any word, phrase, or action that the submissive or bottom (or even the top) can utter or do that causes whatever is going on in the scene to stop or pause. Agreed-upon safe words are taken very seriously; if a top is caught ignoring a safe word, they are often ostracized, if not outright banned, from the community.

People use whatever they feel comfortable with as safe words. But most people use the universally accepted red/yellow/green.

- GREEN: "Everything is just peachy and I'm having a good time." You generally wouldn't use this unless the top leans over and whispers, "How are you doing?"

- YELLOW: "What you are doing is not so great and you should probably switch to another activity unless you want me to say 'red' in another minute."

- RED: "Stop the scene completely now!"

If the submissive cannot speak during the scene (because she is gagged, for example), a common mechanism is for the top to give the bottom a toy or bandana to drop if they need to stop.

Using "no" as a safe word is not recommended because some of us like to say, "No, please, no, stop!' when we really mean, "Yes, yes!" For some, saying no is often part of acting out the fantasy.

There are people who like to boast that they don't use safe words at all. Sometimes it's because they believe they know each well enough, both their limits and their body language. Certainly, first-time play with a new partner is totally different than with a committed partner who knows you very well. Some believe that safe words are silly; simply talking with your partner should be sufficient. While I think that is true, I still believe that safe words are a good idea.

Safe words give the top or dominant a clue as to what's going on with the submissive in all regards, mentally and physically. To refuse to use a safe word in the appropriate circumstance is like getting in an airplane, blindfolding the pilot and saying, "Okay, now take me where I want to go."

There are times when safe wording is not just appropriate, but a necessity for trust and growth. That is why it is vital that partners discuss the use of safe words (or "pleas for mercy," as my own master prefers) and the circumstances when they are needed.

A safe word is only as dependable as the person you're playing with. A safe word will not magically make a bad dominant stop. It is simply a useful tool for making sure a good (or at least decent) dominant/top understands when you are in distress.

Chapter 20: Know Yourself

Okay, you've figured out what turns you on, but have you thought about *why* it turns you on?

It's not necessary that you are able to point your finger at a specific memory or life event and say, "Aha! That is why I am submissive!" It is, however, important that you spend some time examining your personality, strengths and weaknesses, and thinking about your reasons for seeking this lifestyle.

You need to be sure you're doing this for the right reasons.

- Because the idea of being someone's property excites you, not because you don't think you deserve anything better.

- Because being called "whore" and "slut" in the bedroom makes you hot, and you know that's the only reason your partner calls you those names; not because you believe, deep down, that you are every bad thing those names imply when said as an insult.

- Because you know that you have so much to offer the person who has earned your trust and devotion, not because you think that doing absolutely anything asked of you is the only way to earn someone's love.

- Because you want to enhance your life and grow with a compatible partner, not because you're afraid of being alone.

Those who come to this lifestyle hoping to find a magic cure for what ails them usually find themselves disappointed and ultimately more confused. Worse, they may find themselves easy prey for others drawn to the lifestyle for all the wrong reasons, those who will only exploit their broken parts and make it even harder for them to trust themselves and know their own value.

It only makes it more confusing to consider that some (not all, but some) have felt broken and incomplete in vanilla society because there is something deep inside them that is simply *different*.

Not bad, not wrong: just different from the path most people choose to tread. Our needs run deep and wind through the very core of us. Until we confront those needs, and embrace that difference, we will always feel that something is missing.

If you are one who has those needs and hungers for the "right" reasons, just knowing that there are others who feel similar things will help you feel more comfortable in your own skin and more accepting of yourself.

I say "right" reasons for lack of a better term. Some have been so battered and twisted by life that they have come to loathe themselves, and seek pain, humiliation and degradation because they feel they deserve no better.

They come to believe that if they will let people do terrible things to them, or if they are good enough in blind obedience, then finally — finally! —someone will give them the love they so desperately crave. These are understandable reasons, but not healthy ones for giving your body and soul to another person.

The question is: which came first? Yearnings for things you didn't understand that made you feel broken? Or bad experiences and people in your life that broke you, so that you began to think submission, pain or servitude was either what you deserved, or the only way you could earn love? In other words, submission became a default survival behavior, not a choice.

Early in my life, I realized I had an enormous capacity for devotion, to give myself to someone with an intensity that could rarely be reciprocated. And which each failure, I felt worse and less loveable.

I wondered what was wrong with me. Why did I need to give so much, and why I was getting so little in return? My life as a submissive and slave has taught me that I simply am wired differently, and that level of devotion and obedience in me is not wrong or bad or unnatural, it was merely a facet of my personality looking desperately for the right person to give itself to.

Like many others, I always had dark fantasies that made me wonder what was wrong with me. But my sense that something was wrong with these fantasies was juxtaposed with the seemingly opposite knowledge that I *did not deserve* to be treated in those painful, degrading ways. I knew I was intelligent, witty, caring, capable and responsible: a good and decent person. So why on earth did I want all those "bad" things done to me?

Finding the kink community gave me the valuable insight that I was not the only one who'd ever felt such yearnings. I learned that the things I wanted were not "bad" in and of themselves.

- Kneeling or crawling is not bad, if done for the right reasons, in the right time or place, with the right person.

- Being called a "whore" and a "slut" is not bad, if you know that the person calling you those names does so with affection and because it excites you both.

- Licking someone's boots is not bad, if you feel moved to do it to show your love and devotion.

During your journey as a submissive, you will shed many of the restrictions and norms that society imposes on us. You will need to examine these acts in an objective light, to find out how you feel about them, not what the world tells you to feel. There is enormous power in that.

If you choose to explore sadomasochistic play, you'll learn things about yourself that most people never do. People spend their lives fearing and avoiding pain. When you stand before your master or mistress, accepting and enduring pain, you realize that your body is far more resilient than you knew. When you overcome some of the most basic human fears, you experience an enormous sense of satisfaction, self-confidence and strength.

Our hungers are not something sick that needs to be exorcised, but something requiring courage to embrace, to explore, to harness and control. The more you are able to accept these yearnings, to explore them in sanity and self-awareness, the stronger you will become.

Submissives have a natural urge to give service, devotion and obedience to someone. We simply have to make sure that someone has earned it by treating us with respect, care, compassion and understanding.

Think carefully about why you want this. Be painfully honest with yourself. Are you strong enough to do this? Can you stand up for yourself and say no when you mean no? Can you walk away from people who aren't acting in your best interests?

The weak and broken have no business playing around with BDSM. What we do is a powerful magic. If you have other problems in your life, such as addiction to drugs or alcohol, and picking the wrong partners over and over again — please, please, please: seek counseling and work on getting yourself to a healthier place before entering into a D/s relationship.

If you can't say *no*, your *yes* has no value.

Kate Kinsey

Chapter 21:
Dispelling the myth of abuse

One of the most persistent and damaging myths you'll hear from the vanilla world is that if you like this kinky stuff, you must have been abused as a child.

Absolutely not true. There is no correlation whatsoever between BDSM and having been the victim of abuse, sexual or otherwise, in childhood. I know a huge number of kinky folks who had near idyllic childhoods, including me.

But like any other group of people, there will be those who *did* experience some form of abuse, but that does NOT mean the abuse made them kinky. Sadly, child abuse is simply so widespread. Many, many more survivors turned out to be conservative vanilla heterosexuals.

Some kinky folks with past sexual abuse do find BDSM instrumental in reclaiming their sexuality. Sexual abuse robs people of their natural right to a healthy and happy sex life. Because BDSM relationships focus so strongly on honest communication and value consent above all, many are able to rebuild their ability to trust within our community. They can learn to enjoy their sexuality on their own terms.

If you have been the victim of any kind of abuse, you're the only one who knows whether or not you're in a place where you're ready to explore submission. Just know that your past does not make kink inevitable, nor does it mean that you can't enjoy it in a healthy, well-adjusted relationship.

There may be some types of play you might choose to avoid. I've known submissives that simply could not tolerate being beaten with a belt: it triggered too many memories because a belt was what their parent used to beat them. Rape victims may not be able to deal with rape play, though I've known some who specifically used it to work through that trauma. Just pay careful attention to things — be it types of play or even just words or phrases — that make you uncomfortable.

BDSM can help you build a bridge and get over it.
But crossing it is always your choice.

Chapter 22: What's the difference between a submissive and a slave?

Well, if I had a dime for every time someone asked this, I'd be writing this on a laptop from a beach somewhere in the Caribbean. If you venture out into the world of online BDSM discussion groups, you will find this particular question being debated, argued and fought about with ridiculous and mind-numbing frequency.

New submissives ask this question a lot because they're trying to find out where they fit in this community. A lot of people scorn labels, but the fact is that labels give us a starting point for a conversation.

So what is the difference between a submissive and a slave? I could begin by telling you what others might say, or have said:

- A submissive is someone who negotiates; a slave does not have that right.

- A submissive has limits; a slave has given up all limits except those that his/her owner sets for them.

- A submissive obeys and serves by choosing to do so each time and retains her will. A slave initially makes a choice to obey his/her master/mistress at all times and then submits to the will of his/her master at all times.

- A submissive accepts submission, while a slave accepts obedience.

- A submissive has retained some rights within the context of the D/s relationship, whereas a slave has given up all rights and becomes, in effect, property.

- A submissive is owned, but a slave is possessed.

- A slave is not allowed to sit on furniture or wear clothes, and always kneels at his/her owner's feet.

- A submissive has a safe word to end play, while a slave has consented to "no consent."

- A slave must be a submissive, but a submissive is not necessarily a slave.

- Being a submissive is just a step on the way to the "ultimate" state of submission, which is being a slave.

- A slave is more submissive than a "mere" submissive. Submissives are just playing; slaves live the lifestyle.

- A submissive has more self-respect than a slave. Slaves are crazy, because who in their right mind would want to be a slave?

Yada yada yada.

This is about the point where the fist fights and hair pulling begin, until someone tosses the ultimate Holy Hand Grenade of Judgment: "You're not a *real* submissive/slave!"

All of the above definitions are something I've actually heard people say, or read in various books or websites. Some of them are things I've believed myself at one time. Some of them are completely true for the way a particular person lives, functions and perceives himself or herself as either a slave or a submissive.

Some of them are pure poo. (*Read this carefully:* the list above is NOT to be taken as fact, but only as an example of some of the things people will say.)

We get further asking what a submissive and a slave have *in common.*

Both have a deep need/desire to submit/surrender/give up at least some part of their will/control/power to a dominant.

They most often need this because pleasing and/or offering service to a dominant that has earned their trust, their respect and (generally) their love, is an integral part of a submissive/slave's fulfillment and satisfaction.

So if we follow this common ground to its natural conclusion, then a submissive and a slave are really the same except for the extent to which they submit. A slave submits more of themselves (all of themselves?) to their owner.

Ah, but what is *more?* What is *less?* And who decides?

Just like that, we're back in sticky territory because everyone wants to quantify and measure the degrees of submission and dominance.

Visualize everyone on a big sliding scale: dominants on one end, submissives on the other. On the far end of the dominant side are the masters and mistresses, whose personalities and needs to control compel them to take on the added responsibilities that come with owning either a slave or a submissive.

On the other end would be those with submissive personalities, needs and desires. (I differentiate between *desire* and *need*. Desire is a luxurious word, a word of craving, as in a "desire for chocolate." I've never heard anyone say that they desire food, but always that they *need* food. A need is reserved for something you cannot do without. The more a submissive *needs* to submit (as opposed to merely desiring it), the further out on the scale they go. The more control they need to surrender, the closer they come to slavery.

Are you still with me?

I chose the phrasing of that last sentence quite deliberately: "the *closer* they come to slavery." True slavery cannot legally exist in this country — and none of us would really want it to.

Even if an individual agrees in every imaginable way to "be" a slave, there is no court in the United States that recognizes slavery, consensual or otherwise, as a valid status.

If that slave decides to stop being a slave, there is no legal means to force them to return to that state, even if they signed a dozen notarized documents and have their owner's name branded on their ass.

If leaving is an option, then is it really slavery? What we call slavery in the kinky community is a carefully crafted and maintained *fantasy*, even if it is fuelled and compelled by very real needs, and lived 24/7 in very extreme states of control and obedience.

The sliding scale theory works until you start trying to make marks to represent the measure of submission or dominance in an objective, rather than subjective, way. A yardstick works because somewhere, someone, once upon a time, decided that a certain amount of linear space is called an "inch" and everyone else agreed to adopt this objective unit of measure.

But there is no comparable measure for our lifestyle; there is no inch, centimeter, foot or yard. Certainly not one that everyone agrees on!

My master and I created a presentation for a college class of social workers; we were educating them on the basics of BDSM and kink, so that when they encountered it in their work, they would know how to recognize the difference between consensual BDSM and domestic violence. We tried using a linear scale to represent the broad spectrum of sexual expression.

On the Power Point slide, I placed a sweet little picture of nun on one end marked ABSOLUTE CELIBACY. On the other end, I placed a photo of a manly dude decked out in full leather and chains, brandishing a riding crop. Then, we began laying out the behaviors in between the two. After the nun, I put MASTURBATION, followed by HEAVY PETTING and ORAL SEX, then HETEROSEXUAL – MISSIONARY – POSITION – SEX –

WITH – THE – LIGHTS - OUT.

"But not everybody would put oral sex before typical intercourse," Sir remarked. "Why did you put it there?"

"Bill Clinton," I remarked dryly, thinking myself very witty. "I read somewhere that most teenagers today don't even think a blow job is having sex."

And it kept getting more and more problematic with every sexual activity we added. ANAL SEX? Do you put that before or after EXPLORATION – OF – THE - ENTIRE – KAMA - SUTRA?

I know some women in BDSM that can take being beaten bloody, but they will *not* have anal sex even with their husbands. And if you consider gay and lesbian orientations, then the placement of anal sex, oral sex, fisting and the use of dildos are going to be different than where a "normal" heterosexual might rank it.

You can't put SWINGING before SM — or vice versa — without either group howling in outrage if you imply either behavior is more extreme or far out than the other. (Many swingers think BDSM practitioners are sick and twisted, while many in the BDSM community still hold monogamy as a gold standard for "decency." And in case you're unclear about this, BDSM and swinging are not the same thing, not even close.)

In the end, we admitted that a linear chart of sexual behaviors couldn't be anything but the broadest generalization, not to be taken literally. The placement of each activity is potentially different for *every single person in the world.*

What is kinky to one person is "normal" to another. It's the same problem with my attempts to make a scale for dominants and submissives.

You can generalize the end points of the scale, but there is no way to measure the degrees in between because every single person in the kinky community is measuring according to their own yardstick. One person's inch is another person's mile.

One submissive may find being naked in front of strangers is a huge amount of control to give up — for her.

But another who considers himself a slave may feel the nudity isn't a big deal at all.

Another "slave" may consider breath control a hard limit, while another "submissive" enjoys breath play and does it regularly.

For a long time, I considered myself a slave, because that was what I wanted to be, and what my master desired me to be. I accepted polyamory and swinging, activities which some others who *also* considered themselves slaves would not condone in their own relationships.

While I allowed my master to control how I dressed, what toys he would use, even whether I would breathe or not, there was always one area that he never attempted to control, and I would have been really uncomfortable and unwilling to give up: that of my personal finances. Yet many slaves believe that you cannot be a "real" slave if you cannot give over complete control of all areas of your life, including your money.

But even in my vanilla relationships, including an eleven-year relationship where we owned a home together, we never even *discussed* a joint bank account. If you consider this one area of my life, there are a million married vanilla women who are more "slaves" than I have ever been, or ever will be.

I mention these specifics to demonstrate how many variations and levels there are, not just in the kinky community, but also in life, period. Every role in the BDSM community is eventually tailored, like a fine suit, to fit the individual as they grow, evolve, and discover themselves and what works for them.

The identity of your partner will further tailor your particular suit. While your suit may look a lot like someone else's, it will never fit anyone else in quite the same way. So why do we keep trying to pull roles off the rack for other people, sometimes even ourselves?

The minute you start trying to define what makes one person *this* and another *that,* you start comparing. When you compare two things that are not exactly same, you will always find one or the other lacking in some way.

But that "lack" only has meaning in the comparison to that other object. Every other thing in the world will be less or more, depending on what you compare it to. You may like one better than the other, but that doesn't make an orange any less "real" or valid than the apple.

If you continually compare your life — your mind, your heart, your soul — with someone else's, there will always be something that makes you feel less or more, somehow lacking or superior.

In both cases, you are paying more attention to what someone else *is* or *isn't* than rejoicing in what you *are.*

With comparison comes judgment, which can only be based on a personal viewpoint. You cannot unplug yourself from what you know and feel and experience. Judgment is the first step towards prejudice, stereotypes and intolerance. All of which is antithetical to a lifestyle that is based on the need for personal expression and rejects being forced to conform to society's view of "normality." We all came here to be what we are, not what anyone else told us we should be.

In my journey, I was a slave because that was what I needed and wanted to be. That is what my master needed and wanted me to be. It was an ideal we were both striving for, not a definitive state we would ever be able to achieve. *Submission* did not seem a strong enough word for us to contain all the needs and fantasies we both brought to our relationship. So we chose other words — Master and slave — that seemed to convey our goals more clearly.

Whether those words meant the same thing to anyone else was ultimately beside the point. Who should really care whether I, as "slave," sat on the furniture or not? Kneeling or standing, my heart was the same. We were tailoring our leather skins to fit us, not anybody else. And why should we? Those skins were ours, and we would never ask anyone else to wear them.

In the end, my personal conclusion is simple. Submission is a personal journey, always fluid. Slavery, while "generally" the more extreme end of submission's sliding scale, is more useful as an ideal some strive for. And it doesn't really matter in the end. What is submission to you may not be submission for me. What is slavery for me may not be slavery to you. The only definitions that matter in your life are your own, and the person(s) you serve.

We are, ultimately, the only ones who can decide who and what we are. I began this path to find me, not someone else. I departed from the vanilla norms because those skins did not fit me, not merely to find another set of standards to conform to.

So don't worry about the difference between submissive and slave. It's purely up to you and your partner to decide. Stop poking about other people's wardrobes and concentrate on constructing your own.

Choose the material that most appeals to you, the pattern that fits you best. Then alter it, take a snip here and tuck there… Let out a seam if it binds; embellish it with all the spangles and ribbons and colors of your fantasies.

And wear it with pride. It's a one of a kind.

When it comes to submissive/slave arguments, save your breath. The chance that you'll succeed in changing anyone's opinion is about the same as teaching a dog to type.

Chapter 23: Information

It's a very good sign that you're reading this. You'd be surprised how many wannabe submissives go running out into kinky traffic without reading anything but *Fifty Shades of Grey*.

The more you know, the more confident you will be when you venture out into the kink community. Knowledge also makes it less likely that someone can take advantage of you. While I am grateful (and flattered) that you have chosen to read *my* book, my advice is to read a couple more. Here are just a few I recommend:

- *SM 101: A Realistic Introduction* by Jay Wiseman

- *Screw the Roses, Send Me the Thorns: The Romance and Sexual Sorcery of Sadomasochism* by Phillip Miller and Molly Devon.

- *Come Hither: A Commonsense Guide to Kinky Sex* by Dr. Gloria Brame

- *Domination and Submission: The BDSM Relationship Handbook* by Michael Makai

- *The Ultimate Guide to Kink: BDSM, Role Play and the Erotic Edge,* edited by Tristan Taormino

There is a mind-boggling amount of information available on the Internet, so much so that it's hard to separate the good information from the bad.

Before the Internet came along, people had to place ads in magazines found in adult bookstores, and exchange snail mail before anyone actually met anybody else. It was hard to even figure out what it was that you wanted, let alone to find other kinky people to do it with.

Today, you can just type a word into Google and — bam! — there are books, videos, websites, services, stores, clubs, toys, news articles, blogs and podcasts at your fingertips in the privacy of your own home.

Anybody can throw up a website claiming to be the world's greatest dominant. There are guys out there right now who have posted their "2,078 Golden Rules for the Ultimate Submissive." There are women who claim to teach you all the secrets of how to find the dominant of your dreams; you just have to give them your credit card number.

DON'T BELIEVE EVERYTHING YOU READ. For every knowledgeable, experienced and honorable person on the Internet, there are two more with absolutely no fucking clue and one more with malicious intent.

There are several big social media and dating sites out there, with more popping up every day. I'm only going to talk to you about one, because in my experience, it's the only one that matters: FetLife.com.

A bit of painful honesty:

If you're too busy to learn all you can about BDSM before you put your life in someone else's hands, you're not smart enough to play these reindeer games.

Kate Kinsey

Chapter 24: FetLife.com

FetLife has succeeded where many social media sites have failed, becoming "the Facebook for kinky folks." It is predominantly heterosexual, though it is open to absolutely everyone with an interest in kink of any kind.

A large part of FetLife's success lies in its refusal to put advertising dollars ahead of its members. If you compare it to other sites, you'll notice that there are far fewer ads, and those that are there do not dominate the page. The site has a laid-back and good-humored attitude that doesn't take itself too seriously.

If you are not already on FetLife, you need to be. If you're not ready to talk to anyone yet, you will still find an enormous amount of information there. You can simply read what others write in their profiles, their journals, what they post in their photo albums, and in the more than 70,000 different discussion groups.

As of August 2014, the top five groups on FetLife are:

- **Novices and Newbies** (142,000+ members)
- **Kinky and Geeky** (132,000+ members)
- **Submissive Women** (88,000+ members)
- **Curvy Women and the People Who Love Them**

(85,000+ members)

- **Under 35** (83,000+ members)

There are also groups for submissive men, for masters and slaves, for rope and bondage enthusiasts, book clubs, toy makers, polyamory, BDSM on a budget, BDSM-related humor, art and erotica. Within each group, there are thousands of active discussion threads on just about any subject you can imagine. You can also search by place for kinksters in your area, as well as any groups and events near you.

Nothing is perfect, and FetLife has its fair share of trolls and drama queens looking to pick a fight, but mostly it's very friendly and very helpful.

I've been on those other sites, and all that I ever got out of them were emails from guys looking for free blow jobs and a few other really creepy things that made even me go "Ewwww." Seriously.

Welcome to the dark side. Have a cookie.

Chapter 25:
Jumping In (or Coming Out)

So, you're just about ready to step out into the kinky community. How exactly do you that? This is where FetLife comes in again. It's simply the biggest, best and easiest-to-use tool to make the transition.

Many people are happy to pursue BDSM strictly online, either through chat rooms, email or Skype. Because so much of BDSM is mental and emotional, valid and fulfilling relationships are possible, and it is certainly a safe way to get your feet wet. For some people, online is enough.

Most of us, however, want something more.

Step 1: Create a profile on FetLife:

- Don't put your real name out there, but try to be more creative than just Slave999999. Think of something you feel comfortable with, but that captures something of who you are — or who you want to be.

- Remember the basics of Internet safety and common sense. Be careful how much real information you post. Things like your birthday, your address, and your workplace should not be used where strangers can see them.

- Don't use a recognizable photo of yourself unless you are comfortable with the entire world seeing it. Many use a photo that doesn't include their face (a pair of sexy boots, for example), or an avatar of some kind.

- If you want to post a naughty photo of yourself, be aware that the more explicit the photo, the more suggestive comments and emails you will get. If you're okay with that, go for it. But don't post a photo of yourself with a cock in your mouth and one in each hand and be surprised if you get all kinds of offers from strangers. You'll get offers either way, but you'll get more (and ruder ones) with an explicit photo. It shouldn't be that way, but it is.

- Don't post too little, either. When someone looks at your profile and sees that you've made no effort to post anything at all, they may assume you aren't really serious about being there.

- Besides, you're more than just a kinky person, aren't you? Mention your other interests, the music or movies you like or your hobbies. It will help people with similar interests find you. You aren't just looking for a partner, you're looking for friends.

Step 2: Find your area. At the very top of every page you'll see a menu bar. Left to right, it reads *Fetlife, Kinky & Popular, Groups, Places, Events* and *More.* Click on "PLACES" and then on your state. FetLife will then show you lists of:

- People living in cities and towns within your state

- Events scheduled in your state

- Discussion groups on FetLife potentially related to your state

- Cities, towns and regions within your state for further exploration

Step 3: Join the discussion group(s) for your area. If there isn't one in your town, you may have to expand your search to a town or city nearby. Make sure you look for statewide groups as well. If there is a BDSM club in your area, they will usually have a discussion group of their own as well.

- No, you don't have to join them all, but join at least one. You might poke around a bit and see which one has the most members or the most posts. (Sometimes a group dies and no one bothers to take it down.)

- Take a moment to read *About & Rules* (located just under the name of the group). It will help you make sure you start off on the right foot, and don't misunderstand or violate some protocol of the group. Many have a policy that asks members not to post want ads for partners. There is a specific group for those kinds of posts.

- Underneath *About & Rules*, above the lists of discussions within the group, you may see a bright red tab that says *Sticky*. This is a kind of Post-It note of helpful information. Stickies often contain answers to the most frequently-asked questions in the group. READ THEM.

- Just hang out and "listen" to the conversations for a while until you feel comfortable. You will learn a lot, and when you ask a question, you will get feedback from all kinds of people. Just remember, many are wonderful, experienced people, but some of them are just idiots. (I wish we could make those people wear labels, but so far I haven't been able to get funding for the idea.)

- You don't have to limit yourself to local groups. You can also look for the groups that are of specific interest to you.

Step 4: Be prepared to get a lot of attention. When a new submissive posts a profile, a lot of dominants will come sniffing around. It can be a bit overwhelming.

- Try not to get caught up too fast in intense conversations with potential dominants. You really need to find friends first; finding a dominant can wait until you've got your feet firmly on the ground.

- Be wary of any dominant that seems too aggressive. If someone emails or messages you constantly, or pushes for a meeting, or wants to "collar" you or "mentor" you right away, these behaviors are often red flags for someone who is potentially bad news. You can block them from messaging you again or even seeing your posts.

A little further on, we'll talk about dominants, what to look for, and what to avoid. That subject is a chapter all by itself!

Find friends first. At this point, you need friends more than you need a dominant or a play partner.

Chapter 26:
What's a munch and how do I find one?

A munch is a very casual, informal and very vanilla get-together at a local restaurant or bar. It's usually the first step into the kinky world, and the safest way to meet people in your area.

Everyone is expected to dress just the same as if they were going out to dinner with their family, and to behave "normally." There is nothing to identify the group as anything other than just a group of friends having a meal together. Nothing is expected of you beyond simple good manners and an openness to getting to know other like-minded people.

If you are nervous about going alone, email the munch organizers and introduce yourself. The organizers are people who are dedicated to helping people start their journey in BDSM and they are always happy to help. They can tell you what to expect and answer any questions you might have. You'll feel better knowing at least one person there.

Finding a munch near you

You will find posts about munches in the FetLife discussion

groups for your area. Depending on the size of your town or city, there may be more than one munch happening on a monthly basis. Often there are munches specifically aimed at people under 35 (TNG, or "the next generation" or FYK, "fresh young kink") or just for submissives. Most, however, welcome everybody equally.

There's also a very useful website called Findamunch.com, which lists munches all over the country. Be sure to check it out as well.

If you go to your first munch, and find you are too nervous to get out of the car, don't beat yourself up. This happens to a lot of people. It's a big step, after all. Just don't give up; try again next month.

If your first munch isn't a huge success, stick with it. All too often, a newcomer is disappointed that they don't make best friends that very day — or worse, they look around the table and don't see anybody that looks like their ideal dominant — so they don't go back. Relationships of any kind take time, and you have to make an effort to interact with the people you meet.

The munch will introduce you to the people who make up your local kinky community. Not everybody attends munches, but most do, at least occasionally. If there is more than one munch in your area, it's helpful to attend them all at least once, because you'll find different munches attract different audiences depending on time, location, and the personalities of the organizers.

When you attend your first munch,
you'll be amazed at how "normal" everyone looks.
Just like you.

Chapter 27:
The importance of the local community

I can't emphasis this enough: make friends *first* in that local group before you think of finding a dom. Particularly reach out to the experienced submissives of the same sex and/or orientation to help you navigate. You'll need someone to bounce thoughts and questions off of, and it needs to be someone who isn't trying to get inside your panties.

There are many benefits to making friends in your local community:

- You'll find out about parties, clubs and other events where you can experience play in a safe environment.

- You'll find out about educational classes and demonstrations that are very important for learning about safety and types of play.

- You can get references about local doms that approach you, and warnings about those you might want to avoid.

- Predators seek out newbies who are isolated and without a support network; being a part of the local community lets those that might be tempted to take advantage of you know that others are looking out for you.

- If you run into a problem, you will have a support network in place to help, especially if something happens that you are hesitant to discuss with your vanilla friends and family.

**Making new friends around whom
you can be yourself is a wonderful thing.**

Chapter 28:
The "dark side" of the local community

BDSM groups are really no different than any other: churches, book clubs, alumni associations, charity groups, etc. The more people you bring together, the greater the likelihood that some of them aren't going to play nice together. Sooner or later, every group has its fair share of personality clashes, power struggles and just plain cattiness.

When you gather a bunch of dominant personalities, some of them are going to compete for power or conquests or reputation; they may not even realize they're doing it, but the negative effects are just as damaging.

And it's not just the dominants that compete: the submissives can be as bad if not worse. You'll find that many groups are actually organized and run by the submissives, and some of them can be pretty dominant when it comes to getting things done they way they think it should be done.

Mix in the complicated dynamics of couples hooking up and then breaking up — often while one or more former partners is still playing in the same dungeon club! Stir in the even more complicated dynamics of polyamorous relationships and "leather families," and it's simply impossible for there not to be occasional bad blood and hurt feelings.

Bottom line: remember that people are people. Some people will bad-mouth others with very little real knowledge.

If you are warned about someone, don't ignore it, but don't swallow it whole before you get a better sense of whom you're talking to.

**Remember the lessons of kindergarten:
play nicely with others.**

Chapter 29:
Dungeons, clubs and play parties

Most large communities will have a local club or dungeon/play space where kinksters get together to socialize and play. These places aren't for everyone, but they can be enormous fun.

Every club has its own rules, but most are private, meaning that you have to be invited by a member, or screened in some way, before anyone will even tell you where it is. Reasons for this include:

- Protecting the privacy of its members, who may not want everyone in town knowing they're kinky.

- Protecting the club itself from "tourists" who just want to "see the freak show," and members of the media looking for a sensational story.

- Keeping a low profile to avoid scrutiny from law enforcement and politicians. Most clubs are fully licensed and completely legal, but the conservative environment of many communities still make our clubs vulnerable to people operating on misinformation and ignorance. Many a politician looking for votes has targeted "adult entertainment" and other "vices." No one wants to be raided by the cops or picketed by local churches.

Clubs are great for those people who can't play at home because of children, thin walls or lack of space. Not everybody has the room or disposable income for their own private dungeon. Clubs have a wide variety of wonderful equipment to be enjoyed: crosses, whipping posts, cages, swings and real exam tables for medical play.

Not everybody who goes to the club on a Saturday night actually uses the play equipment, however. Many people simply go to socialize with their friends and meet new people. Some go because it gives them a chance to dress up in their wildest, sexiest clothes. Others attend because it's a place where they can truly be themselves; masters can lead their slaves around on leashes, and submissives can kneel naked at their dominant's feet.

Communities that don't have a club often have play parties in private homes or in a rented space like a hotel ballroom or banquet hall.

Most clubs have a cover charge, membership fee or suggested donation to help cover the operational costs, but it is almost always staffed by volunteers. Often you are asked to sign a waiver and show proof of your age. Minors are absolutely forbidden; depending on the state, the legal age may be 18 or 21.

One thing that surprises a lot of people is that many of these clubs and parties do not allow alcohol. There are two reasons for this. First, many feel that alcohol or any other substance that can impair judgment or sensation is not safe for BDSM activity. Secondly, the presence of alcohol makes getting an operating license much more complicated and opens the club to other legal issues.

Every club has its own policy about how much sex and nudity is permitted. These rules are not about prudishness, but safety and local laws.

Allows honor the rules of any club or party.
The rules are there to protect you and everyone else.

Kate Kinsey

Chapter 30:
Why *you* should go to a club or party

Clubs and play parties are wonderful education opportunities for novices. You will not only meet more people, you can observe all kinds of play and play styles. Afterward, you can ask questions of the top and bottom, and you can learn the safe way to do things. Reading books and surfing the web can be very educational, but nothing is better than seeing it for yourself.

Many new submissives make the mistake of thinking they don't need to know how to actually *do* any of this. After all, they aren't planning to tie anyone up or flog someone, so why bother learning how?

So that you will know when someone is doing it *wrong* to *you*.

Having that knowledge will give you the confidence to speak up when you're not comfortable with the way a top is going about something.

Dungeon monitors

Most clubs and parties will have *dungeon monitors*: experienced tops and bottoms that move around the space observing all the play. They intervene if they see someone in serious distress, or about to do something stupid. If you go to a party, ask who the monitors are. Introduce yourself and tell them you are new. They will do their best to keep an eye on you throughout the night. They may even be able to suggest the best scenes to watch or people to talk to.

The benefits of public play

Public play is certainly not for everyone, but exhibitionism is a popular component of kink for many people. Some submissives find it deeply satisfying to show their obedience and adoration for their dominant in front of everyone, just as some dominants enjoy showing off their submissives.

You don't have to play in public, and even if you do play, you don't have to do it completely naked. Remember, everything is negotiable!

One of the unexpected benefits of public play is becoming more comfortable and accepting of your own body. You will see people of all ages and sizes enjoying themselves. While some people will always be shallow enough to judge others based on their looks and weight, most people in the kinky community tend to be far more accepting of those who do not resemble Barbie dolls.

Unless the idea of playing in front of other people is just too traumatic for you, a play party is the best place for you to experience your first play. You'll be among friends who can watch out for you. Just the fact that people are watching generally makes every dominant just a little more careful to stay well within your limits.

Don't be surprised if you don't react quite the way you expected. You never know just how your mind and body will react to something you've never done before. When you play in public, there are more people around to help if you need a little extra support, aftercare or simply have more questions than the top can answer by himself.

**Even if you don't think you'll be playing with anyone,
ALWAYS wear nice underwear to a party...
just in case you change your mind!**

Kate Kinsey

Chapter 31:
Playing well with others

Different people approach play in different ways.

Some people will play only with their significant other. Others will play with lots of other people, too, though they may have different limits with others than they do with their partners. Many will play, but certain sexual acts, genital contact and exchange of body fluid are off limits.

You may find a married dominant that wants to play with you, but only with his wife (or submissive's) knowledge and/or permission. It all depends on the negotiated boundaries of their relationship.

Some have open relationships, where both (all) parties agree that even intensely sexual play is okay within certain agreed-upon limits.

Some are polyamorous, which means that the partners have intimate, loving relationships with more than one person at a time, with the knowledge and consent of all parties. Naturally, they will play with some or all of their partners. Some poly people play only with the partners in their "house" or "family," but others also engage in casual play with other people.

Some are completely monogamous. They play with their partner and no one else, ever.

Some single doms and subs play with as many different partners as they can manage! Again, the limits involved vary with every negotiation.

As an uncollared (unowned) submissive, it is perfectly acceptable for you to play with whomever you want. Playing with different tops or dominants is a vital part of the learning curve, and one I highly recommend. Just remember that you are the only one who sets your limits. You are not required to have sex of any kind with someone just because you play with them. Don't let anyone tell you otherwise or pressure you into anything you aren't comfortable with.

Once you are collared or serving a dominant in some capacity, you will obviously need to negotiate whether or not you are allowed to play with others, within what limits, and whether his or her express permission is allowed. Some dominants jealously guard their submissives from being used by anyone else; another will love to "loan out" his property (sometimes just because he knows his sub likes it!)

**You don't have to be in an intimate relationship
with someone just to enjoy casual play.**

Chapter 32:
Aftercare, subspace and sub-drop

Ah, subspace! It's that altered state brought on by the body's release of endorphins and/or adrenalin during play that most submissives seek like the Holy Grail. Most describe it as a highly relaxed floaty or dreamy feeling. It's very much like being stoned or drunk, but it's a natural high produced by your body.

Just as different people react differently to drugs and alcohol, not everyone reacts the same way to subspace. Some lose physical coordination, their reflexes are sluggish, and coherent thought is difficult. Some are just a little giddy or tired.

Some submissives go so deep into subspace that they lose the ability to speak or respond. Obviously, those who experience that depth of submersion have to be very careful because they lose their ability to safe word, and they may not even know when they have sustained serious injury.

You may experience subspace all the time, some of the time, or you might not experience it at all. Many sadists deliberately prevent their submissives from reaching subspace, because the deeper the submissive goes, the less pain she feels. The sadist very much wants the pain he inflicts to be felt.

You may find you don't react the same way every time you play. So much depends on your physical and mental state going into the scene: how much sleep have you had, are you well hydrated, when did you last eat? Certain medications like antihistamines can also affect your reactions.

My own reactions range from the overwhelming urge to curl up and sleep, purring like a kitten, to walking around grinning like an idiot looking for something — even stale crackers — to eat. But I have, on more than one occasion, simply burst into tears though everything went very well.

Sub-drop

Now, if all of those hormones and chemicals rushing through your body can produce such a wonderful, blissful state, it's not surprising that they can create *another* kind of reaction when they leave. We call it "sub-drop."

Like subspace, not everybody experiences it to the same degree, and some don't experience it at all. Sub-drop can occur immediately after a play, or hours later, or the next day, or the next week. Your body has to rebalance all those hormones, and that is why the timing of sub-drop can vary greatly.

Physical symptoms include:

- Exhaustion
- Shakiness or weakness
- Feeling cold
- Thirst

But there can be emotional symptoms as well:

- Sadness
- Confusion
- Insecurity
- Anger or irritability

Just knowing that you are not experiencing something out of the ordinary helps a great deal, but the most effective prevention for sub-drop is *aftercare*.

Aftercare

Aftercare is the treatment given to a submissive or bottom after play is over to help them return to the real world. A good dominant or top will either provide aftercare, or arrange someone else to provide it if they cannot.

Aftercare can include a number of things:

- Wrapping up in a warm blanket
- Affectionate, comforting words
- Cuddling and hugs
- Rehydration
- Eating (if you have diabetes or other blood sugar issues, make sure you discuss this with your play partners)
- Comparing notes about the scene
- Any necessary first aid

- Sex (if that is within the parameters of the relationship)

As you learn your own tolerances and reactions, you'll learn what you need in regards to aftercare. Some need little, some need a lot, and it can vary according to how intense the play was. Other submissives just want to be left alone to decompress. I've known a few submissives who just needed to cry, even if the scene was fabulous and they were ecstatically happy.

You are entitled to whatever kind of aftercare you need. If you play with someone rude enough (or just plain ignorant enough) to run off immediately after the scene is over, ask a friend to sit with you for a bit. Don't get up and try to pretend you're fine if you're not. People will understand.

 Even with a casual play partner, there is an intimacy and a bond that doesn't turn off the moment the flogger stops swinging. Both top and bottom benefit from taking a moment to enjoy that connection; abruptly walking away from each other can be emotionally jarring.

Top-drop

Keep in mind that a top often needs aftercare, too. They work hard and expend a lot of energy; they may have been standing during an hour-long scene and worked up quite a sweat. They need to sit and drink some water or fruit juice.

They also need to be told they did a good job. Even if the scene wasn't the best ever, you can usually find something nice to say about some part of it. When play ends, a top can feel guilty for doing such terrible things to someone, and hearing "thank you" helps a lot.

A good top or dominant should also check in with the submissive or bottom the next day to make sure everything is okay. It's a simple gesture of caring that goes a long way to helping the submissive (and the dominant in many cases) avoid sub-drop.

Providing your own aftercare

If you find yourself exhibiting symptoms of sub-drop the next day or even several days later, there are things you can do:

- Take a deep breath and remember that you are not crazy, that what you are feeling is normal, and it will pass.

- Reach out to an understanding friend. If that person isn't kinky, you don't have to explain sub-drop; simply tell them you've had a bad day and need some sympathy. If they can come over and give you a hug, or meet you for a cup of coffee, great. If they can't, then a chat on the phone or online can help.

- Pamper yourself. Take a bubble bath. Take a nap. Watch a favorite movie with a cup of tea.

- Cuddle up with your dog, your cat, your old teddy bear, your favorite sweater.

- A little treat like ice cream or chocolate is good, but don't over do it. Heavy starches and sugars can often just make you feel more sluggish. Don't starve yourself either. The goal is to help your body get back in balance.

- Same goes for alcohol. A glass of wine: yes. A bottle of wine: no.

- Exercise. It really can alter your mood and help you feel better.

- Write it out. You'll find that keeping a journal will be beneficial in many ways for many reasons.

The scene isn't over until the aftercare has been given.

Chapter 33:
Finding a dominant
(or just a play partner)

All right, you've studied up on terminology, limits, safety and your own desires. You've made some friends you can trust, and you've been to a few munches. You've been to a couple of play parties and observed some amazing stuff you're just dying to try.

You are now ready to start looking for a dominant of your own, or at least someone to play with.

Most of what I advise is more about protecting yourself than finding a dominant. Protection is important because you'll need to take care of yourself until you do find the right dominant for you.

Most of the mistakes and heartache I've seen in new submissives arise primarily out of being so eager to find a dominant that they jump into things too quickly. Take your time; the dominants that try to rush you and push too hard are usually not the ones looking for a serious, lasting relationship. Be on the lookout for some of these common red flags or warning signs.

Red flags to watch out for:

"I want to collar you now."

Seriously? Do you really want a dominant who throws out collars like Mardi Gras beads? What would you think of a guy who offered you an engagement ring on the first date?

What you need is a dominant who takes things slow, who wants to get to know all of you — not just your body, but your heart and mind — and someone who makes careful, thoughtful decisions about something as important as this.

"I don't want you talking to other dominants."

Many predator dominants prey specifically on isolated submissives. So don't isolate yourself – and don't let a dominant isolate you.

Don't let yourself be tricked into believing that he's protecting *you*. He's protecting *himself*, because if you talk to someone else you're either going to realize he hasn't got a clue or he's violating some major ethical points.

A good dominant will encourage you to learn as much as possible, from as many people as possible.

"If you were a true submissive, you'd do what I want."

Whenever anybody talks about a "true submissive" or a "true dominant," it makes my skin crawl. The people who talk about "true" anything are usually the ones who won't listen to (or respect) anyone else's opinion, and they are oh, so eager to pass judgment.

A good dominant will understand that everyone has to find his or her own comfort level, and that no one should be rushed. They also know that being a submissive does not mean you are submissive to everyone, even them.

"You must have no limits to be my slave."

In other words, he is looking for someone so naive and/or desperate that she will jeopardize her own health and safety. Do you really want to belong to someone who values you — or any submissive — so little?

And if, when you balk at this, he says he means that you'll have no limits except those *he* sets for you, thank him kindly and walk away. Your limits are yours, always. You have a right to them.

If you ever consider entering into this kind of agreement, it should only be after someone has earned your trust over months, if not years — not demanded it within days of meeting you.

"You don't need a safe word with me; I don't allow them."

He may also say that he's so good at reading submissives, a safe word is unnecessary. No one is good enough not to need your honest communication. This translates as: "I don't care about your feelings or your well-being. I don't want to know if you are injured or in emotional distress."

Beware of anyone who:

Insists on a private first meeting: in a hotel room, or his home or yours.

Expects or insists on playing at the first meeting.

Expects or insists that "play" include sex if you don't want it to.

Other ways to protect yourself:

- **Learn the basics of safety** and don't be afraid to speak up if you are uncomfortable with something that seems to violate any of those basics. RUN from anybody who says, "I have plenty of experience, who the hell are you to tell me I shouldn't wrap this rope around your throat and leave you bound and alone for a couple of hours?"

Bondage seems like a fairly simple type of play, doesn't it? You simply tie someone up and do whatever seems like fun. But the most injuries in BDSM involve bondage, probably because it *does* seem so harmless that people get careless.

We had a famous case here in Tennessee, where a couple was playing around with bondage. It's not known whether they had done any research online or at the bookstore, but it was certain they had never sought any education in BDSM safety precautions within the local kinky community. The husband ended up dead. The wife left him bound and alone, and he died of positional asphyxiation (when someone's body position keeps them from being able to get enough air into their lungs).

There is a right way to tie someone up, and a wrong way. There are ways to be prepared when something unexpected happens. That couple found out the hard way that you NEVER leave a bound person alone.

Unfortunately, you can just as easily find someone within the kink community who may have been practicing BDSM for some time, who hasn't bothered to educate themselves in safety, and they can put you in risky situations just as easily as the inexperienced. This is why educating yourself by reading, talking, asking questions, and getting to know as many people in your local BDSM community as possible is so important, so at least you know the way it should be done so you can recognize when it's wrong.

- **Learn to say NO.** It is your right and obligation to yourself — and whomever you eventually decide to give yourself to — to protect yourself from harm, mental and physical. If you cannot say "no," your "yes" has no value. No respectable dominant wants a doormat.

- **Never meet anyone in private**, only in a public place; always tell someone where you are going and with whom. The best safety practice is to take a chaperone along with you. (Sigh. I know 90% of you will never do this but I say it anyway.)

- **Play the field** before committing to one person. You need experience to find out what you really want and need.

There are so many different varieties and styles of BDSM, and there is no one "true" way to do it. Group play parties are especially good settings for this.

- A **"mentor"** who wants to have sex with you is not a mentor.

- A **"protector"** who wants to have sex with you is not a protector.

- Beware of those who want to **"train"** you. Don't fall for the idea that there are these magical "trainers" running around out there who will help you find a master/mistress. They won't. They just want to have fun with you. If you want to have fun with them, go for it! It can be fun to be "trained," and you can gain a lot of experience that way; just don't let anybody make you think you *have to*. "Training" is not something everyone does because there is no universally accepted set of skills or behaviors. (More in a following chapter.)

**Don't be so desperate to find a master
that you accept the first one to come along.**

Chapter 34:
Different types of dominants

You will find many types of dominants out there. Some of them will turn you off, others will appeal to you. Sometimes it's just a matter of personal style and philosophy, not something they are consciously trying to be. This is by no means a complete list, and many dominants may exhibit elements of more than one category:

The Daddy Dominant:

The Daddy dom wants a "baby girl" to pamper, spoil and/or discipline, to guide and take care of. He is nurturing and kind, but he can be strict. His BDSM relationship may incorporate elements of age play (where the submissive enjoys being a "little" that behaves like a child) or may not.

Why would anyone want to "be" a little? Children are (mostly) free from stress, worry, and the need to make decisions. They feel safe and cherished. Children play with simple yet wildly imaginative exuberance, with coloring books, pixie sticks, tea parties, juice boxes and story time. You may want to recapture all those feelings from a wonderful childhood — or finally get the nurturing you didn't get in real life.

A Daddy/baby girl relationship is not about incest — though you will find those fantasies out there. (I don't judge anyone for their fantasies, only for their actions.) But many if not most of the daddy/baby girl kinksters don't go there at all. Some don't even include sex in their relationship in any way, shape or form.

There are mommies and little boys, but Daddy/baby girl relationships are the most common. And remember that not all Daddy/baby girl relationships include age play or anything related to childhood at all. Sometimes, it's just the "feel" or style of the relationship.

The White Knight Dominant:

He's a protector dom who wants a cherished submissive/slave or even his own princess to protect and care for. Think chivalry, duty, and honor. He wants to be your hero in every way. If you are looking for romance, the White Knight is your best bet.

My only concern with White Knights is that sometimes they get sucked into lost causes, trying to save someone who either doesn't need to be saved, or doesn't want to be. He's definitely a fixer, and that can be both good and bad.

White Knights can also be problematic because in trying to protect every submissive in their world, they give some submissives this false belief that they *need* to be protected, i.e. that they are not strong enough to stand up for themselves.

The Hunter/Predator Dominant:

This is difficult to explain, but I'm going to risk it. In the midst of all my warnings about consent and respecting limits, many of our fantasies still center around a dark, mysterious and slightly frightening stranger who sweeps us off our feet and does terrible things to us.

I call them hunter/predators, though I don't mean predator in the sense of someone who victimizes, abuses, misrepresents and psychologically damages. I mean predator as in a hunter. One who prowls.

The big bad wolf. The pirate. The outlaw. The bad, bad boy.

Because we fantasize about being prey, don't we?

Of course, it's imperative we remember that in our fantasies, we are still in control of everything that happens. In fantasy, you decide where and when and how it happens; you are only hurt exactly as much as you want to be hurt, and not a second longer than you want it. Absolutely nothing in your fantasy happens that you don't consent to.

Some dominants are really good at tapping into those kinds of fantasies. They are good at playing the role of a predator or sadistic bastard who likes to scare you just a little. They are often experts at setting the mood through mental imagery. As much as we want our limits to be respected, there is still something very exciting about a stranger leaning in close to you, without any introduction or negotiation, and whispering in your ear, "I'd like to do terrible things to you."

You don't find much discussion about this kind of dominant, mainly because it's so hard to explain the difference between a fantasy role player and a dangerous sociopath. It's easier — and safer — for me (and everyone else) to tell you to simply run from these guys.

That's the downside of safe, sane and consensual; it can severely limit spontaneous and deliriously exciting seductions that just happen. Fear play uses adrenalin, and it can be intoxicating, but it requires that you really *be* afraid, at least a little.

These aren't bad guys; they simply have the *fantasy* of being one, just as we have the fantasy of being ravished by them. They are often exactly what we're looking for.

How do I know this?

Because the hunter/predator dominant was exactly what I was looking for when I started this journey. I met a lot of very nice, "respectable" dominants that talked to me about consent and negotiation, and they left me cold.

Then I met a hunter/predator, and he was everything I ever dreamed about. He made all my fantasies come true.

Thirteen years later, he's still my master and my best friend.

Hunter/predators walk a very fine line between being the best thing that ever happens to you, and being the worst. Because not everyone understands or appreciates this style of domination, the hunter/predator is often met with disapproval by some members of their community, while others respect and admire them. Sometimes they get bad reputations that are completely undeserved. Sometimes they get in trouble because they misread the signals and attempt to seduce the wrong kind of submissive, one who doesn't enjoy that kind of fantasy.

Consent violations can happen in any kind of relationship, and are no more or less common with the hunter/predator type.

Be aware that these dominants are out there. Handle with extreme care, but don't write them off as dangerous psychopaths. He may just be a sheep in wolf's clothing.

How can you tell if he's a good guy? Ask those who have played with him, not just those with opinions. There are women my master played with fifteen years ago who still call him long-distance to get advice about their newest partners, and others who take him to lunch when they pass through town. In fact, I've never met anyone who's actually played with him that doesn't think he's a great guy and a wonderful dominant.

The Fresh Meat Dominant:

They are the ones particularly turned on by newbies, for a variety of reasons:

- He may be totally inexperienced — sometimes dangerously inexperienced, even within our community — who desires you because you won't know just how inexperienced he is, and he will lie rather than admit the truth. It's not wrong or shameful to be new at this on either side; it *is* reprehensible to misrepresent yourself and not be actively trying to improve your knowledge, sharing the learning curve honestly with your partner. Avoid this one because he can really hurt you. (And when/if he does, he will run for the hills faster than you can say Safe, Sane and Consensual.)

- He may be a wannabe: one who isn't really a dominant at all, but just a guy using it as an excuse to get laid by someone whom he thinks is easy, and willing to do stuff his wife or past girlfriends wouldn't. Some of these guys thinking being dominant means unlimited blow jobs on demand. Avoid him, because he's not interested in meeting your needs at all.

- Then there is the truly experienced dominant who seeks out fresh meat because it is a rush for him. Your inexperience excites him, because he loves the thrill of introducing you to all the sensations. He gets to experience that initial delight — something he may have lost — vicariously through your joy and passion. There's really nothing wrong with this, if he is honest and upfront about what he is offering you: fun, excitement and experience, but very likely no possibility for a lasting, significant relationship. He probably already has a submissive partner and has no intention of trading her for you. Often these dominants are the best teachers; the problem lies in the risk to your heart.

The Gorean Dominant:

I must admit that I have a hard time with this particular type of dominant, largely because the first Gorean master I ever met at a party refused to speak to me. I didn't understand why he kept snubbing me in such an unfriendly way until someone said, "Don't worry about it; he's a Gorean."

Goreans are people who attempt to fashion their lives and relationships on a series of science fiction novels by John Norman. (No, I am not making this up.) First published in 1966, the Gor novels (over thirty of them) feature a parallel universe with lots of military action (reminiscent of Rome and other ancient civilizations) and sexual adventures. The world order on Gor is primarily male dominants and female slaves. It is a highly ritualized, protocol-driven, 24-7, TPE (total power exchange) that, in my admittedly limited experience, tends to take itself way too seriously.

I also find it to be highly misogynistic because it suggests that *all* women are — or should be — submissive to *all* men.

That's why that first Gorean master wouldn't speak to me. I was too far below him to even merit his attention. Some Goreans, I'm told, don't even consider themselves part of the BDSM community.

Another thing that annoys me about Gor is that Gorean slaves are expected to refer to themselves in the third person. She never says "I would like to serve you," but "This girl would like to serve you."

I tried to read one of the books a long time ago, but it was so bad I was afraid my eyes would start bleeding. If you find that Gor appeals to you, I wish you nothing but luck and happiness. I know it's wrong to make fun of anyone's choices but, try as I might, I just can't take Gor seriously. It offends me as a feminist and a writer.

Now, if you'll excuse me, I need to go batten down the hatches because I am going to get a lot of hate mail from the Gorean community.

The Service Dominant/Service Top

There are varying opinions on what constitutes a *service dominant.*

Some consider a service dominant one who is more top than dominant; he or she enjoys delivering activities like spanking, flogging or bondage because he/she knows his partner enjoys it. His/her payoff is the bottom's pleasure, and in the strictest sense, he or she isn't a dominant at all.

Some do consider themselves dominants to their primary partners, but play with others in the capacity of service top. Service dominants/tops make excellent teachers and mentors.

Most of the service dominants (or tops) I've known are rather like kindly uncles. They are interested in you both having a good time, without much or any D/s elements.

If you find yourself turning out to be more of a bottom than a submissive, a service dominant/top could be just the ticket.

The Creepy Dominant:

In the kink world as well as the vanilla one, some people are just plain creepy. Often, they make your skin crawl, or make you uncomfortable in some way, even when you can't quite put your finger on why.

As with any community, the kinky world attracts its fair share of misfits with poor social skills. The idea of being dominant unfortunately appeals a great deal to people who just cannot get their shit together.

These are the ones who ask inappropriate questions, talk about extreme or bizarre fantasies, don't respect your personal space (if you are unlucky enough to run into them in person) and will stalk you online or, in some cases, in real time.

Trust your gut instincts. Don't think you have to be polite because you're "just" a submissive. Don't give them the benefit of the doubt. If he makes you uncomfortable, that's all the reason you need to walk away.

You're not just looking for the right dominant; you're looking for the right dominant for *you*.

Chapter 35:

Protecting your heart

We talk a lot about protecting our bodies and our health as submissives, but not so much about protecting our hearts. In reality, it's usually our hearts that sustain the most damage.

The Catch 22 of D/s is that submissives have a built-in tendency to go absolutely mad for the dominant who takes us on this wild, intoxicating ride. Our appetite for them is enormous, and the more we submit, the more control we are willing to give up to them. We don't intend to fall in love with them, it just happens.

It's also a sad fact that our first experiences seem so earth-shattering, we can't imagine that the other person doesn't feel the same intense connection. But often they don't.

If you are playing with an experienced dominant, odds are that he's been down this road many times. He's been through that honeymoon period of D/s — that intense connection, the passion and excitement that can only come in the very beginning of the relationship — with various partners before.

In polyamory circles, you'll hear it referred to as *NRE: new relationship energy*. Simply put, it's that first flush of infatuation that happens in vanilla relationships as well, but in BDSM relationships, it can be far more dramatic because we play with more intense sensations and dynamics.

This can lead to a good bit of pain for the submissive when she realizes that she and her dominant partner are not soul mates who are going to spend the rest of their lives in a 24-7 fantasy.

Sometimes, it is just a lot of fun, pleasure, affection and friendship. And those aren't things to be sneezed at.

But that reminds me that there is one more type of dominant to watch out for: **the Collector Dominant.**

He has one or more submissives already, and wants to add you to his harem. Again, nothing is wrong with this if you go into it with open eyes, keeping both hands on your heart; dominants have a right to their fantasies, too. But all too often, the submissive finds herself hopelessly entangled in a relationship that's painful, and sacrifices many things she wants for what she can get.

And that is the perfect lead-in for discussing polyamory.

Love is the ultimate submission.

Chapter 36: Polyamory

I've mentioned it already, though technically polyamory has nothing to do with BDSM. It needs to be discussed simply because you'll find so many people in the BDSM community also practice polyamory.

According to Wikipedia:

> **Polyamory** (from Greek πολύ *poly*, "many, several", and Latin *amor*, "love") is the practice, desire, or acceptance of having more than one intimate relationship at a time with the knowledge and consent of everyone involved. It is distinct from swinging (which emphasizes sex with others as merely recreational)

Cheating is not polyamory. If he has to keep you a secret from his wife or other partner(s), that's not poly, that's lying. Having sex or playing with someone is not polyamory. Swinging is not polyamory.

Polyamory is about love.

Polyamory can be a wonderful thing, because it accepts the reality that people often experience an intense attraction to someone new, yet does not force you to discard your current partner — if everyone agrees, that is. Done with honesty and full communication, poly can enrich the lives of all involved because let's face it, there is no such thing as too much love.

Unfortunately, I've seen too many submissives that end up in a poly relationship because they fell in love with a poly dominant, and the only way to be with him was to embrace poly as well.

Polyamory can be an intensely painful thing for someone whose heart isn't in it. As much as you may want to be able to be such a good and devoted slave that you accept sharing your partner with others, sometimes it just doesn't work.

Combining poly with D/s

This is my personal opinion, and there are those who would disagree, but polyamory, when paired with D/s, is even more difficult, if not impossible. Poly only works when everyone involved has an equal voice in the relationship. Poly is not about one person saying, "I will have as many lovers as I want and you will accept it." Poly is about everyone involved saying — and really meaning it — "I want my partners to have all the love they desire."

For poly to work, everyone needs to be able to make some compromises. Even a slave has to feel like she has some say in the people she accepts into her life, and that her needs are just as valuable as her master's.

Again, my personal advice: if you find someone who says, "I can be poly but you have to be monogamous" — tell him to kiss your fanny. Unless, of course, that idea somehow, miraculously, turns you on.

Before you find yourself in a poly relationship, read up on what is and what isn't acceptable poly practice. Learn about how good poly relationships work, and all the different types of arrangements that poly can encompass. You have every right to negotiate the poly relationship just as you should negotiate the BDSM aspects.

Like BDSM, polyamory has no one right way to do it except that it must encompass the knowledge and consent of all parties concerned.

If your insecurity has been a problem in your past relationships, polyamory probably isn't going to work for you.

Kate Kinsey

Chapter 37:
A few words on training

Training is one of my pet peeves. I want to track down the person who started this line of BS about training and smack 'em.

"Don't you realize how you're fucking up the heads of newbie submissives," I want to shout at them, "implying that there's some universal guideline of how to do this stuff? That they can be trained like an accountant or hair stylist?"

The thing is, I do know who started it.

Long ago and far away, some kinky folks wrote some kinky books. *Story of O*, the Gor novels, Anne Rice's *Sleeping Beauty* series, and Laura Antoniou's *Marketplace* novels, to name the most well-known.

In these books, writers constructed some elaborate kinky fantasies about slaves and masters. And, because their characters have to *do* something in their novels, some of them made up some interesting rituals of behavior and dress, such as kneeling or sitting a certain way.

Some other people read these books and found them exciting. Some of them even went so far as to say, "Wouldn't it be hot if I had a slave that I could make sit a certain way, dress a certain way, speak a certain way?"

This is how protocol — the use of ritual and rules of behavior in BDSM relationships — was born.

Reality Check:

There is not, nor has there ever been, a real Marketplace where consensual slaves are trained and bought and sold. I have author Laura Antoniou's word on this. She swears she made it all up out of her own splendidly kinky imagination.

Pauline Réage, who wrote *Story of O*, isn't around to ask anymore, but considering that she didn't even *participate* in BDSM activities, I think it's safe to say there is not, nor was there ever, a Chateau d'Roissy for the training of consensual slaves.

Even if there is, somewhere in the highest levels of the ridiculously rich and powerful, a secret society for masters and slaves, the chances that you or I or anyone we know is going to find it, let alone be invited to join it, are about twenty billion to one.

Note: I'm not going to get into a human trafficking discussion here, because we all know that is **not** what we're talking about.

If you run into some dominant who tries to convince you that he is a member of such a society, or that he belongs to some ancient house of dominance and submission in France or Romania or the planet Mars, take him with a very large grain of salt. It is far more likely that these men are lying than that these things really exist.

There is no standard to which you can be trained. There is no board or certification committee that grants some dominants the authority to train submissives. Kinky folk can't agree on all this stuff any more than all *Dr. Who* fans can agree on their favorite doctor, or all *Star Trek* fans can agree on whether Kirk or Picard was the better captain.

So who are these trainers?

There are two types of dominants out there who will want to "train" you.

There's the kind who say they want to train you, when what they really mean is, "I want to fuck you without any of the responsibilities or commitments of ownership, or even an emotional involvement." For them, training is a racket, a scam, for getting as much play and sex as possible. I've heard of a couple that even got submissives to pay for the privilege.

Then there are those who have every honorable intention in the world. They really believe they are helping newbies gain experience that will make them better submissives.

The problem with even the well-intentioned trainer is that, because there is no universal agreement for how a submissive should behave, the only thing they can train you to do is what *they* believe is correct and pleasing.

Your dominant or master, when he comes along, may not find any of that useful at all.

Training also gives the impression that all D/s relationships are protocol-based. Most aren't. High protocol is a specific subset of D/s and, in my experience, the exception rather than the rule.

Training implies there are techniques and skills to be attained. Dominants actually need more specific skill training than a submissive, because no one should just grab up a flogger, a coil of rope, a pair of nipple clips, etc. and start using them on someone without taking some time to learn how to use those things properly.

But if you are a submissive, then you are a submissive. There is nothing to be learned that can make you a submissive if you are not. Submission is mostly about how you react to dominance. Dominance in another person will call out to you, and you will respond in a way that comes naturally for you.

Training could teach you endurance and patience, I suppose. But then, so could yoga. Other than that, there is nothing to be trained in, until you find the right dominant partner(s) for you. Then and only then can someone (your master or mistress) tell you what special areas he or she wants you to be trained in — or not.

No one has ever asked me to "present myself" or engage in any type of special protocol behavior. The vast majority of dominants I've met don't have a checklist of skills they are looking for. They are looking for the one to whom they connect, whom they will then shape into a more perfect complement to their needs. That submissive should have such a connection to that dominant that being shaped to those needs is what they really want.

What "training" claims to accomplish are things that are really the basis of building a relationship. Everything you experience will be richer if it's shared with a person to whom you have an emotional connection.

Not just someone who is "training" you.

You may eventually find a dominant who wants to train you on how to assume certain positions, or how to serve formal tea, or how to bark like a dog whenever he snaps his fingers; but to train for that now, when you may never need it, is a waste of time.

Go out and learn things that will help you grow as an individual in this lifestyle, or things that you'd like to know for yourself. Read, study, observe, and ask questions. Learn the terminology people use, so that you can ask intelligent questions. Learn how it works for different people, so that you can open your mind to all the possibilities. Learn about safety, first and foremost.

Now, if learning to serve formal tea gets you hot, or appeals to you for purely aesthetic reasons, then go for it. Find someone who can teach you that particular skill. It will be a gift you can offer to the one who eventually takes ownership of you. But remember that it may not matter to him or her at all. Your master may value the ability to belly dance or juggle or balance his checkbook more.

You can explore different types of play: to discover what you like, what you don't like, what your bad triggers are, what your good triggers are. Play as much as you can safely, to learn your tolerances. But you don't need a trainer to do this, you just need friends that can be trusted not to take advantage of you, and have the experience not to fuck you up physically or mentally.

Unless, of course, the very idea of being trained is a fetish for you. If you want to pretend you're being prepared for the auction block in the Marketplace, go for it, if it turns you on. I would never suggest you pass up an opportunity to live out a fantasy.

My point is that you don't have to do it. Nobody requires you be "trained." There's no diploma or secret handshake waiting at the end of it.

You don't need training. You need supportive friends, knowledge and self-awareness.

Chapter 38: All those wonderful toys

When you start playing, you will probably want to purchase a few specific toys and equipment. Don't have to get carried away and buy everything in the adult bookstore, but there are some things that you don't want to share with anybody else simply for hygienic reasons.

Leather and cloth, being porous, absorb everything from semen to body oil to sweat to saliva to vaginal fluids to blood. The same is true for most wooden items.

Items for your personal use only:

- Dildos and vibrators
- Clit massagers
- Anal beads and butt plugs
- Gags
- Blindfolds/masks (consider the possibility of eye infections)
- Rope for bondage coming in contact with the genital areas
- Clothespins, if used on genitals; so many people use wooden clothespins because the plastic (and therefore easier to clean) are not as easy to find; if you find plastic clothespins, buy them!

- As you progress to more intense kinds of play, you'll want to consider your own single tail (whip) and canes, because these are toys that easily break the skin.

Every dominant is supposed to know how to take good care of their toys, but not all of them do. Having your own is easier than wondering if the ones belonging to the dominant who just asked you to play are truly cleaned and disinfected. Of course, you can always clean them yourself and put your mind at ease.

You need to learn how anyway, and there is a ton of information online about how to take care of toys. With your own dominant or master, you are often expected to take care of his toys, and to know how to put them away in his toy bag(s) to his specifications.

But it is much safer to play with your own "fluid-bonded" toys even when it comes to floggers (which has many "falls" or tails), whips (which only have one tail, hence a "single tail"), canes and paddles. If you sweat heavily on a flogger — or get scratched and bleed on it — it's almost impossible to get it completely clean. The only solution is to make sure that flogger is only used on you, and no one else. That's what we mean by fluid-bonded: your fluid is on it, it's bonded to you.

Many dominants who play with multiple partners will use a condom on any insertables. It's a good idea to carry condoms with you just for that purpose.

Building your own toy bag

It's also a good idea to begin building a toy bag of your own. Too often submissives depend on the dominant to provide all the toys, but then we miss out on choosing things that we really like. Besides, the only thing worse than breaking up with a good play partner is losing all your favorite toys, too.

Remember that you don't need everything in the catalogue. Some good ideas, in addition to the ones we just mentioned as your "personal use only" toys, to start with are:

- A light- to medium-weight flogger
- A set of wrist and ankle cuffs that fit you comfortably
- At least one paddle
- If you want more than one paddle, choose different sizes, materials, and flexibility
- Nipple clamps
- A riding crop

Your toy bag should also contain:

- A basic first aid kit
- Condoms
- Latex gloves (or non-latex in case you or a play partner has a latex allergy)
- Lube (research the best lubes; do not simply buy the cheapest!)
- Sugary candy for blood sugar drops (an even better choice are the glucose tablets sold in the drugstore)

- Aspirin or the pain reliever of your choice
- Any medications you may personally require for physical conditions
- EMT scissors (used by paramedics to quickly and safely cut through thick materials like seat belts, hence good to quickly release someone from bondage in emergencies)
- Baby wipes
- Breath mints (might as well have minty breath, right?)

You can easily add to your toy bag as you learn what you like. It's better not to buy some expensive toys until someone has used it on you and you're sure you really like it. Some of these more specialized toys include violet wands, TENS or other electrical stimulation toys, single tails, needles, pumps and cupping sets.

Whatever you have in your bag, know how to use it, and how to clean it.

Never, ever offer a toy to be used on you to someone who doesn't know how to use it! A single tail, for example, is one toy that requires a great deal of skill and practice to use safely. Someone who has no experience with a whip can cut you to the bone. (Of course, they'll probably really hurt themselves before they manage to hit you, but don't take the chance.)

You want to buy good toys that will last, but you don't always have to spend a lot. Many events will have raffles, giveaways, and silent auction fundraisers. Many ordinary items like wooden spoons, spatulas and paint stirrers, make excellent "pervertables."

Skip the handcuffs, unless you have some serious cop fantasies. Not only are they a tired cliché, they are highly uncomfortable and can cause nerve injury if worn for extended periods.

Kate Kinsey

Chapter 39: Sub-frenzy

Sub-frenzy is a phenomenon that affects many new submissives. It's that first rush of overwhelming, consuming desire to experience every kind of kink, as soon as possible, often to the point of neglecting all other concerns.

Most of us have thought about submission long before we ever have the nerve to go looking for it, and when we do, it's often like someone dropped a bomb in the middle of our world. You can become consumed by it. BDSM is all you can think about.

Is there really a difference between sub-frenzy and enthusiasm?

Yes, because the particular factors involved can be so intense that a submissive's judgment and instinct for self-preservation can be impaired. You can be really enthusiastic about cooking, but the chances of physical injury from too much baking are pretty slim.

Being enthusiastic and intensely interested is fine; it's when you let that enthusiasm cloud your judgment that sub-frenzy becomes dangerous. In extreme cases, a submissive may risk not just health and safety, but their jobs and family.

Submission involves some very powerful magic, both physically and emotionally. You need to proceed slowly as you learn about your own needs, your reactions, your tolerances and desires.

What are the signs and symptoms of sub-frenzy?

Basically, it's when you're going too fast and taking too many risks. You're doing things that, a year from now, you will look back on and ask yourself, "What the hell was I thinking?"

- Playing too soon with someone you just met;
- Playing too often (you don't take time between plays to process mentally and emotionally, or to heal physically);
- Engaging in types of play that you haven't educated yourself about enough to know what's safe, what's not and or even if it's something you *really* want to do;
- Agreeing to everything, with everybody;
- Failing to ask questions or make any demands of your own;
- Meeting strangers in private, often without telling anyone where you're going or who you will be with.

Some prefer the term *candy-store syndrome* because newbie submissives are like kids in a candy store. We want it all, and we want it all now, and we don't care that we might rot our teeth, or end up with a stomachache, or in a sugar coma.

Why do we believe this frenzy applies mostly to submissives? Don't tops/dominants experience this kind of extreme enthusiasm that could impair their judgment?

No one denies that new dominants/tops can experience their own challenges and lapses in judgment. But the level of frenzy is more acute for submissives, and the factors that cause it are different, for several reasons.

1. Opportunity

It is the submissive, not the top, who is flooded with interest and offers from the moment she first puts a profile online or ventures out to her first munch. Some of the invitations are respectful and helpful, while others may be vulgar or downright insulting.

New tops simply do not have the opportunities that a submissive does. Reality and limited opportunity puts the brakes on most tops. It's hard to fall prey to "frenzy" when you are struggling to find any play at all.

2. Endorphins and altered states

Endorphins, you'll remember, are a group of morphine-like hormones secreted by the brain when the body is under unusual stress, and can induce a kind of euphoria.

A submissive tends to experience profound altered states while most tops/dominants do not, because, obviously, the submissive is on the receiving end of extreme sensation while the dominant is only delivering it. The endorphin high in itself can be addictive and judgment-impairing.

3. A submissive nature

Submissives *want* to let someone else take control, and they *want* to please. While this is part of what makes a submissive so much fun, it also makes it very easy for them to feel like it's not their place to question, or ask or demand. When you add in all the uncertainty of inexperience, it is very easy for a submissive to get in over her head.

This is NOT to say that submissives are naturally victims. But the nature of their desires make it more likely that they can be manipulated, much more so than the top/dominant.

Most new submissives (and even some more experienced ones) are still trying to get their heads around the idea that being submissive does not mean they are submissive to *everybody*.

4. Level of physical risk

We also call it "sub-frenzy" because the submissive/bottom is the one at a drastically more pronounced physical risk than the top. The submissive is the one being struck, stuck, slapped, poked, prodded, shocked, tied up, choked, beaten, dangled, hogtied, blindfolded and otherwise rendered helpless on the receiving end of possible physical harm.

But that's not to say that tops are not at some level of risk from sub-frenzy. This is another reason why it is imperative that dominants be aware of the phenomenon and watch out for it.

How does sub-frenzy put a top/dominant at risk?

A top who plays with someone in a frenzy state may find themselves dealing with a lot of misunderstandings that, even if they don't result in a serious accident, can still result in tears and drama from an unhappy submissive who puts all the blame squarely on his shoulders. At worst, the top may find a policeman knocking on his door, or rumors circulating that he is not a safe player. At the very least, the dominant gets a ruined play that doesn't satisfy anybody.

It is a potentially damaging double standard that some submissives feel they can skip carefree from play to play and leave all the responsibility for safety and education to the top. That's just not true, and it's not fair, and it doesn't lead to better play for anybody.

When both dominants and submissives are aware of sub-frenzy, hopefully it encourages both to communicate as honestly as possible and make better decisions.

How do you deal with sub-frenzy?

Gather knowledge
Just knowing that there's a name for what you're going through can be enormously helpful. It helps to know that you are not actually losing your mind, and that other people have been through it.

Gathering as much knowledge on BDSM in general is also a good idea. The more you know about safety and terminology, the more you know the right questions to ask potential partners.

Build a support system

Find other submissives, either real time or online; join discussion groups; attend munches. First, find friends and THEN find play partners.

Play with friends

Find a trusted friend or service top who can take the edge off your intensity with friendly play to gain some of the experience you want and need. Or you can find local play parties where there are dungeon monitors and other people around to look out for you.

Use "safe calls"

A safe call is a method where you check in with another person who knows where you are going, who you are meeting and when they should expect to hear from you again. If you don't check in at the arranged time, or if you use a pre-arranged code phrase to indicate you are in some kind of distress or danger, your contact person calls for help. A safe call is NOT foolproof, but it's better than no plan at all.

Exercise

It's true. You can get an endorphin fix from aerobics or kickboxing or whatever form of exercise you enjoy, or (let's be honest!) any exercise that you can stand to do.

Keep a journal

Write it out! Journaling will also be very useful in processing the emotions that go along with BDSM play.

Follow the signs

Take a sheet of notebook paper, then get a magic marker and write, in great big letters, SLOW THE FUCK DOWN. Tape it to your bathroom mirror.

Don't rush it.
This is the good stuff, the magic time.
Make it last as long as you can.

Chapter 40:
More about safe words

We already covered the basics of safe words: what they are, and how to use them. But when you begin to actually play with other people, you need to look at them again in greater depth.

Remember that a safe word is appropriate when something unexpected or unusual happens in either a physical or emotional sense that could take the play in an unexpected direction.

Extreme Physical Reactions

A person who feels that they are about to pass out and is not able to get their head down can actually go into convulsions. In some kinds of bondage, when the bottom is standing, loss of consciousness in which the body goes limp can dislocate a shoulder or wrist, or even cause strangulation if there is anything in the proximity of the throat.

Shortness of breath and loss of feeling in body parts can indicate any number of possible problems, including heart attack and stroke. (And if you think those last two are unlikely, all I can say is that I've had a top experience a stroke in the middle of a scene.)

Then there is **pain that simply does not feel "right."** Blows can accidentally hit the spine or the kidneys. Dildo penetrations can hit the cervix or, anally, perforate the bowels, an extremely deadly accident.

There are a number of much more minor problems that will still ruin a play: sudden paralyzing muscle cramps come to mind. (I remember falling to my knees once and twisting a previously dislocated kneecap, feeling my patella actually shift. That was *not* good pain.)

Emotional and Psychological Issues

Then there are **emotional triggers** that can do as much or more harm than anything physical, and that's another area where hard limits are nothing to be dismissed, abused or scorned, by either party. Submissives have to know and admit their limits because they are part of who we are as individuals.

In the beginning, I personally had a hard time with the concept of safe words on two different levels, and I've found that my issues were fairly common.

First, I did not want the ability to stop play with a word. I was going so deep in my submission that I wanted even that control taken from me.

Some don't want to use a safe word because they feel it puts the real power in the hands of the submissive. How can you submit to someone when you know you can stop the scene with a single word? It's a paradox that can really sabotage the mindset you're aiming for.

My master and I found a way around this that worked for us. I was not allowed to safe word, but I was encouraged to *beg for mercy*, which he (supposedly) might or might not grant. By begging for mercy, I was not attempting to tell him what to do or not do, but clearly still communicating the level of my distress. It may sound like a small thing but it allows us both to keep our ultimate goal — his complete control and my complete submission — intact.

The second issue was my own pride. I fell into that mental trap of not wanting to "give in." I desperately did not want to disappoint my master, but neither did I want others to think I was a fluffy bottom who couldn't take hard play.

I had to come to terms with this reluctance to safe word early on because my master had such a reputation of hard sadism. Others who asked to play with me assumed I was unbreakable. They did things they couldn't or wouldn't do with their own submissives; they hit harder and played longer.

In many cases, it wasn't just the assumption that I could take anything, but a lurking fear on their part that I would find *them* too fluffy. But the end result was the same: many of these doms and tops were venturing into new territory with my body as their learning curve. While I am perfectly willing to be a "stunt sub," the importance of clear, concise communication became even more important.

More than once, I stumbled upon a dom/top on a pure ego trip: "Let's see if I can get the big bad sadist's toy to *red!*"

One dominant crowed proudly about the *yellows* and finally a *red* he got from me, until I pointed out to him that it really wasn't anything he should be proud of. Just because I would take something from my master, I explained to him, did not mean I would take it from *him.*

That's the difference between "bottoming" and "submitting." If I am bottoming, *red* comes when I'm no longer having a good time. If I am submitting to my master, *red* or "mercy" only comes when I have come to the end of my endurance.

Some doms/tops who work a lot with newbies will actually try to push a submissive to safe word as a vital learning experience. They have run into that pride issue before, and know that it can seriously damage a submissive if they don't get past it.

A right *and* a responsibility

A good submissive needs to have no hesitation about using safe words, whether their particular issue is pride or having the confidence to use it. What helps many is the realization that using the safe word is not just their *right* but also their *responsibility*.

We all understand the right part because it goes toward the consensuality of play and the overriding need to protect ourselves from harm. But why is it a responsibility?

Withholding any information about yourself mentally or physically is to withhold communication, and communication is paramount in what we do. So is honesty.

Putting the dominant at risk

We tend to place our dominants on a pedestal, but they are only human. There is enormous pressure on a dominant to read the submissive, and to be in complete control of the scene. Even the most experienced dominant can make a mistake or simply be the victim of an accident. If you do not give them complete information, you put them at risk as well as yourself.

You risk their emotional well-being and confidence, because when the play goes wrong, the best dominants can feel enormous guilt. Parents can easily empathize, even when their child has an accident totally beyond their control. Many are perfectionists, and they will be hard on themselves for not foreseeing the unforeseeable. They carry this guilt with them into the next play, and the next.

Few things are worse for a dominant than for someone who trusted them to be in tears and hurting, throwing all the responsibility and blame back on them. It puts enormous pressure on not just the D/s side of the relationship, but on the love and respect between both partners.

You also risk their reputation as a safe and responsible player. Gossip spreads fast, and details get lost or transfigured as the story goes around. What begins as: "Subbie A hadn't eaten all day, so she passed out during the scene last night with Master X" can easily and quickly become: "Master X beat Subbie A until she passed out! I'm never playing with him!"

The most damaging thing about gossip like this is that no one seems to ever go to the sources and ask for the real story. The rumors and assumptions just collect at the bottom of the community subconscious, until everything else is filtered through the lens of misconception.

When you don't safe word appropriately, you also risk not giving your dominant the pleasure he or she was seeking in the first place. They wanted a good satisfying play, not to have the submissive go into shock, convulse, or curl into a fetal position at their feet. They wanted to see you beaming through happy tears, kissing their boots, deliriously grateful — not drive you to the emergency room.

When you trust your dominant partner enough to know that you can use your safe word, you give them greater freedom, because they know they can trust YOU to be honest at all times. They can experiment with new techniques, new toys, etc. because they have you as an ally, not just as a mute, accepting victim.

In a D/s relationship, all that you are belongs to your dominant; to withhold information vital to his/her judgment of any situation is forbidden. Because you belong to them, one of your first responsibilities is to protect his/her property. If his/her car had a flat tire, you wouldn't just let him/her go on driving, would you? No, you'd tell them about it.

Telling them that a tire is flat doesn't mean you are controlling or manipulating them; it means you are looking out for their property. It is up to the dominant to decide what to do with that information. A good dominant will give the flat tire the attention it deserves, so that the car can continue giving him/her the performance they expect from it.

Usually this is the point when someone will say, "But what about the possibility that the submissive will abuse the safe word?"

You should never use a safe word as some kind of "Get Out of Jail Free" card just because you want your dominant to use your favorite toy instead of his. That kind of behavior is what people mean when they talk about "topping from the bottom," when the bottom or submissive tries to manipulate the dominant.

One way to discourage a sub from misusing the whole safe word concept should be the understanding that safe wording has consequences. I knew a dom who explained to me that if I used my safe word, all play would cease immediately, and that I would be expected to get dressed and go home. Further, he said, we would not play again until we had thoroughly discussed my reasons for safe wording.

With my master, I knew I had better have a damn good reason for asking not to do something. Usually the punishment for inappropriate use of a safe word was not even necessary; my submissive heart was thoroughly crushed by just the look in my master's eyes.

On the flip side, however, I have seen the pained look in his eyes when something went wrong and I did not use my safe word, as he examined a bloodied nose or caught me limping the next day. I've had him hold me and comfort me, praise me for my efforts, even when I did use my safe word and felt as if I'd let him down. Nothing can replace the intimacy of totally honesty between dominant and submissive, and that intimacy is not possible without a complete discussion and understanding of safe words and their usage.

Some couples, when they have played together long enough and learned each other well enough, will tell you they no longer use safe words. That is a personal choice they have the right to make, but it is really a bad idea for those just beginning to explore their own desires and limits to not use a safe word.

You will also find some people who dismiss safe words as silly. "I don't need to use safe words with my dominant," says Sally Super Slave. "We just talk to each other!"

That's fine and dandy; talking is always good. But I can tell you from personal experience that sometimes an occasion will arise during a loud or very complex and active scene, that you just need a simple, uncomplicated and impossible-to-mistake word to signal that you need help of some kind.

Most submissives have a hard time making themselves use a safe word, because the last thing they want to do is disappoint their dominant. Other submissives may go so deeply into a trance-like state of what we refer to as "subspace" that they are physically unable to speak at all. These are two things the dominant or top needs to be aware of, and why beginning slowly when you are new to this is so important. Until you've played a while, you don't know how you're going to react.

Red Flag Alert:

If you are talking to a prospective partner who insists that his submissives may *not ever* use a safe word, watch out.

At best, he's a poor choice for you as a beginner. You can't try new things and learn your limits if he will not allow you to stop play that isn't working for you. At worst, he may be the kind of dominant who forces a submissive into a nonconsensual situation. Many tops play safely and well with no safe words; but if a dominant insists on no safe word, it is sensible to be extremely wary.

You should also be wary of any dominant that becomes angry with you for using a safe word. To discourage the use of safe word is to risk bending consent and to risk damaging submissive's trust. In other words, a dominant who resents you for using a safe word is not a good dominant in the first place.

**Three important things to remember:
communication, communication, communication.**

Kate Kinsey

Chapter 41: The Feminist Submissive

Every woman with half a brain who approaches BDSM as a lifestyle choice has asked themselves the same question: how can any modern woman — let alone a card-carrying feminist — embrace submission?

Well, at first you feel kind of weird about it. Maybe a little guilty. Then you do some long, hard thinking about the paradoxes that populate and define BDSM. Such as, the dominant is supposed to be the one in control, but the submissive can stop the play with a single word; so who is really in charge?

You do some more long, hard thinking about who you are, what you want, and what makes you happy.

You think about the fundamental thing at the very heart of feminism: the right to choose your own path.

Fifty years ago, a woman being spanked over her husband's knee for buying the wrong brand of coffee was considered completely acceptable. Now, if a wife wants to be spanked over her husband's knee just for fun, it's considered kinky or maybe just a little weird.

Fifty years ago, it was purely a man's prerogative to spank/chastise/beat his wife for deviating from the acceptable norm in any way, or just because he wanted to.

Now, if it's the wife asking for the spanking because it arouses her, and arouses him as well, that element of choice and the difference in the motivation for it changes everything completely. Or does it?

Because, of course, our collective psyche carries all the baggage about what those acts mean symbolically and historically. Most of us understand that we are playing with those stereotypes, and that these often arouse us precisely because, on some level, we are turning those stereotypes and expectations inside out.

A submissive is not synonymous with "doormat." Submission is all about making a personal choice to submit to a particular person, at a particular time, within carefully negotiated limits. To participate in our reindeer games, you must first figure out what you want and what you don't want, and you absolutely must learn how to be honest and clear in your communication about it.

This is how all relationships are supposed to be, but BDSM has made communication and consent its holy mantra. We actually have checklists! Some of us even have contracts!

I think back to my first vanilla sexual experiences, and I wish that I'd had the strength and wisdom to say to my partner: *I want this, not that. More of this, less of that. And can we try X, Y and a little Z?* Because that is exactly what you do before engaging in play of any sort in the kinky world, whether it's a casual scene at the local dungeon or the beginning a relationship.

Unfortunately, some women do come into BDSM without

understanding that being a submissive does not mean you are submissive to just anyone and everyone. Sometimes we have to educate those self-proclaimed dominants who think any and every submissive is his for the taking. Want to start a small-scale war? Just let a dominant man walk into a club and snap his finger at the first woman he sees with a collar around her neck, barking, "Bring me a drink!" It's not her master that will cut his balls off, it's *her*.

I've used "him" as dominant, and "her" for the submissive, but that's simply because that's the particular dynamic that concerns feminism. The female submissive/male dominant coupling gets the most attention from the vanilla world, but it's not the whole of BDSM.

BDSM is NOT about gender roles. Submissive and dominant have nothing to do with male/female. There are many female dominants and male submissives. There are women – straight and lesbian – who submit to other women, men who submit to other men. We talk about dominant and submissive as an orientation, like straight, gay or bisexual. It's not unusual for someone to be dominant with one or more partner, and submissive with another.

I began exploring my fantasies when I was 38. I had been a rebel since college, fiercely independent and determined not to be defined by the men in my life. Yet in my secret fantasies, being dominated by a man in the bedroom really got my juices flowing. (I blame it on a Southern Baptist upbringing. I was intensely curious about sex, but was convinced that I would never have sex until my wedding night. Unless, of course, some dashing, mysterious pirate kidnapped and ravished me. Yes, please!)

When I finally began meeting dominant men, I found myself thinking, "Hell, I'm more dominant that he is!" I nearly put a stiletto heel through the foot of one "dominant" who got a little too persistent one night at the dungeon.

Then I met the right dominant. Not the right dominant for everyone, but the right one for me, and he happened to be male. I'd submitted to several women, and enjoyed it, but the sexual dynamic wasn't quite right. I'd played with several men, and enjoyed it, but it wasn't quite right either... until I found him.

There is something inside me that wants to submit, that gains tremendous satisfaction from it, but it will only come out when the right person calls to it. And when that happens, the floodgates open.

Consider the enormous intensity of emotions that come from play that taps into our deepest, darkest and most primal places, that engages not just the body but the heart and mind.

It's deeper and wider than mere "sex": new sensations that you never knew were possible, exploring the body more thoroughly than ever before, sending adrenaline and endorphins coursing through your veins to heighten every sensation. You are doing things you have always wanted to do but never before dared, things that require more trust and honesty than you have ever shared with another before....

How could I not adore the person who gave me all of that? When I came through whatever he asked of me, and saw his pleasure and pride in me, it was the sweetest satisfaction I'd ever known.

Did I question myself as a woman? Yes. But I got over it. Because isn't the surest definition of a feminist a woman who does exactly what she wants because it makes her happy and fulfilled?

It's tough to admit but one of the things I came to love about D/s was the clarity and simplicity of it.

I'm certainly not arguing for a throwback to 1954, because such clearly defined roles can never work without the wholehearted choice of a willing heart. That was the whole problem with 1954: it was assumed that every woman would be a good little housewife whether she wanted to or not. There was no choice involved at all, not for her and not for her husband, either. Maybe *he* wanted to be the one getting spanked, but he couldn't tell anybody that.

But neither should you think that a D/s relationship means a dominant gets to have his way all the time and the submissive just has to go along with it. The submissive has choices. The dominant has obligations. And every bit of it is open to negotiation all the time.

When I became my master's slave, I willingly made all my thoughts and feelings his property, which meant that it was not my place to decide what to hide and what to reveal. Sounds barbaric? Then consider what it means: none of that silent stewing that people so often fall pray to. I'm not allowed to say, "I'm fine," when I'm really pissed as hell. No sulking allowed.

In the D/s relationship, my responsibility is to be honest and truthful, as long as I express myself respectfully. And he has the responsibility to listen to what I tell him, to be sure my needs are being taken care of, that I feel valued and loved.

In agreeing to be his slave, I agreed to give up the struggle to always be right, and that was a BIG one for me. Not to get the last word. Not to score points with a stinging comeback. No more keeping score of his mistakes to hit him over the head with later. I realized just how much bullshit sexual warfare there had been in my other relationships. To give that up was such a relief!

There is no one correct way to do any of this. Do some masters/mistresses refuse to let anyone speak to their collared sub without their permission? Some do. Mine has always told me that he doesn't require or want such micromanagement, and that he loves me for being an independent woman who can speak for herself. And if he'd wanted to micromanage me, I probably wouldn't have remained his for all these years. The D/s only works when both individuals needs and desires mesh and complement each other.

The whole issue of the collar is a sore spot for many feminists. But there's a vast difference in what an outsider believes the collar to mean, and what it really means to those who practice BDSM. A collar is as much as symbol of commitment as of ownership, the BDSM equivalent of a wedding ring, for those who take it seriously.

What has made *Fifty Shades of Grey* and other BDSM erotica so popular is exactly the same thing that brings women to BDSM in general. It's arousing to think of being swept away by passion, to be so desired by someone that he wants to "take" you and "own" you. It's exciting to break the taboos and walk along the edge of naughty.

But none of it would be at all exciting or arousing if your own choice wasn't at the core of it.

BDSM is all about choice, power, pleasure and self-realization. This is my choice, my path, and I see no contradiction as long as I consent wholeheartedly.

Kate Kinsey

Chapter 42:
Privacy and discretion

For so many years, kinky folks have lived in fear of being "outed" — having their sexual inclinations made known to family, friends and neighbors. It wasn't just an issue of embarrassment, but the possibilities of criminal charges and loss of employment, friends, professional standing and custody of children. In many cases, kinky folks were even hiding this part of their lives from their own spouses; being outed could end their marriages as well.

For some of us today, those issues still exist to some degree. Just how much you have to worry about depends on your age, where you live and what you do for a living.

Naturally, people who live in larger metropolitan areas find it less of a problem than someone living in a small town. A single person in their twenties will be less concerned than a middle-aged soccer mom with two kids. Someone working at the corner coffee bar has less to worry about than someone who teaches school or holds a medical license. Even in some corporate jobs, employees sign a "morality clause," which basically means you can be fired for any activity your boss deems immoral or even just potentially embarrassing to the company. (If you work at Hobby Lobby or

Chick-fil-A, quit right away.)

I know a few people who still cannot bring themselves to tell their spouse that they like to be spanked, tied-up or covered in whipped cream while singing "The Star-Spangled Banner." Their kink is kept entirely, desperately secret. It's a terrible way to live.

Child custody is probably the single largest concern, aside from simple (if still painful) personal embarrassment. People can and do lose their children because one parent outs the other as a "pervert."

What happens in Kinky Vegas...

For all these reasons, discretion is still considered one of the most sacred trusts within the BDSM community. If you see someone you know at a local club, or recognize his or her photo on FetLife, you are honor-bound to keep it to yourself.

Like Vegas, what happens in the kinky community, STAYS in the kinky community. Next to violating a safe word, the absolute worst sin you can commit is outing someone, even if you do it accidentally.

This also applies to running into someone you know from the kinky world at the grocery store or (heaven forbid) a PTA meeting. **Do not approach them** unless you know absolutely they are okay with it. They might be with friends or family that have no idea they are kinky, and you might put them in the potentially awkward position of explaining who you are and how they know you.

Some people use scene names or their online screen names at kinky gatherings. I've known some people for ten years without ever knowing their real names. With others, we've reached a level of trust so I not only know their names, but where they live, what they do, and in some cases, I've met their kids and parents, but almost always with the understanding that the kinky stuff is safely compartmentalized.

I have some friends who are completely out of the kinky closet. Going to barbecues at their house is interesting because there are usually a few completely vanilla folks standing in the corner looking a little confused and nervous. (And by the end of the night, at least one of them has asked for an invitation to the next dungeon party. It never fails.)

With today's social media, discretion gets more complicated. For example, I have two different Facebook profiles: one kinky, the other vanilla. Some of the same people are friends on both pages, but we make sure to keep the kink separate from the vanilla stuff.

At least we try. More than once, I've screwed up and posted something on the wrong page. Luckily, no one noticed! But I've also had to rap the knuckles of a friend who posted a totally inappropriate comment on my vanilla page.

Why does it matter to me? Well, I also write nice vanilla books, and my agent thinks it would hurt my sales to be known as a pervert. My mother knows that I'm a "little kinky," and that I call my "boyfriend" *Sir*, but she doesn't want anybody else to know, and I don't want to embarrass her.

In any and all cases: be very careful about what you put out on the web! That stuff never, ever completely goes away and there is no way to know when or where it might turn up again.

At some point, you're going to wonder if you should (or if you can) tell vanilla friends and family that you're kinky.

In most cases, it isn't anybody's business, and there isn't any reason you should bring it up. You wouldn't tell your parents (or your adult children) about the specifics of your D/s relationship or your love of bondage any more than you would tell them which sexual position you favored when you were vanilla.

Then again, maybe you would. I am always amazed at what people decide to share with the world. And if you have a history of sharing everything with your mother or sister or uncle or best friend, keeping something that is such an enormous part of your life secret can be very uncomfortable.

Only you can decide when and if and to whom you want to share your kinky interests. Most of the time, people are not nearly as scandalized as you think they will be.

Talking to your current partner

If, however, you have come to this place while in a vanilla relationship, without your partner's knowledge, I strongly urge you to talk to him or her. You will probably be surprised to find them open to at least exploring some of the possibilities. I've never met anybody who didn't have some secret fantasy they were afraid to share; chances are good that your partner has one or two that they'd like to share with you, if only they dared.

There are places on the web and books with advice about how to discuss your kinky desires with the people you care about. Trying to explore BDSM while keeping it a secret from your partner doesn't work. Trust me.

Been there, done that, got the divorce papers to prove it.

Kate Kinsey

Chapter 43:
Who the heck is Kate Kinsey,
and why is she writing this book?

So, who the heck am I, and why do I think I can tell you anything? It's not that I'm smarter than you. It's just that I've done all the stupid stuff already.

I've had these desires since childhood, but I never knew that anybody ever did anything about it. When I did find out about S&M (as most people referred to it then), I thought it was something the porn industry had made up.

In college, I met my first dominant. Problem was, we had no discussion about it; things just happened. When it was all over, I didn't know if I'd just had the most exciting sexual experience of my life, or if I'd just been date raped. It was confusing, to say the least.

But I never forgot that experience. In my late thirties, when I discovered the Internet, I started looking for that dominant again. I didn't find him, but I did find a lot of information, and a lot of people who shared my interests.

I have been very involved in my local community since I dove into this lifestyle nearly 14 years ago. I was a guild member for Rose-n-Thorn (Gatherings), Nashville's first continuously-operating dungeon space. I have worked as education director for the National Leather Alliance-Nashville and the Mark, the local dungeon. I also do graphics work for the National Coalition for Sexual Freedom (NCSF), an organization I wholeheartedly support.

Through it all, I've participated in dozens of online groups, chat rooms and discussion boards. I've attended a lot of conferences and contests where I've met some of very people whose books first educated me in BDSM.

For many years, I co-presented a seminar to graduate students in social work at a local university, explaining what it is that we do, in hopes that when they are out in the field, making decisions about people's lives, they will be able to separate myth, fear and stereotypes from reality.

Recently, I've been working with KinkyCast.com, a new podcast that explores all things kinky. I've had the pleasure of talking to several people that I greatly admire: Dr. Gloria Brame, who wrote *Different Loving* and other fabulous sex-education books; Laura Antoniou, author of the *Marketplace* series and all-round fabulously wise leather woman; and Ernest Greene, editor of Hustler's *Taboo* magazine and his wife, the amazing Nina Hartley. (Yeah, THAT Nina Hartley!)

I am primarily a fiction writer, with three BDSM-themed novels under my belt so far: *Red*, a procedural crime thriller, and, purely for erotic thrills, *The Totally Uncensored Kinky Adventures of Chloe St. Claire, Sex Slave*: Volumes 1 & 2 so far. Many people contact me through my website or FetLife asking for advice, and that is one of the reason I decided to finally write the book that people have urged me to write for years.

But the biggest reason I've finally written this arose out of an event that was horrific and impossible to forget.

What follows was originally published on my blog in July of 2014. I include it here as a cautionary tale. I don't want to scare you away from exploration, but I do very much want you to understand that there are very bad people out there.

I also want you to remember Shirley Beck as you become a part of our community. Right now, you're the newbie at the local munch or club, but before you know it, you'll be one of the "elders" being asked for advice. Share your knowledge, and be welcoming. There are, unfortunately, a lot of women like Shirley Beck out there. Maybe we can save them. It's too late for Shirley.

Kate Kinsey

Chapter 44:

The Last Four Hours

Of Shirley Beck's Life

Something terrible has happened just up the road from where I live. When the threads online started, I was too sick to even comment. I didn't want to write about it, because what the hell was the point?

But days have passed and I can't stop thinking about the last four hours of Shirley Beck's life.

As I writer, I choose my words carefully, always looking for the best word to convey all the shadings and nuances of my meaning instead of one that is merely adequate.

But we throw around some words so casually that their edges have been blunted. Words like *horrified. Disgusted. Disturbed. Sick. Incomprehensible.*

Those words are pale and tepid, not nearly heavy enough, not strong enough. Using them to describe what I feel about Shirley Beck's death is like trying to smash through a plate glass window with a pebble when what I need is a brick.

Shirley Beck, age 39, was a "house slave" to four roommates, one of whom she called "mistress."

On June 26, three of the roommates beat her to death while the "mistress" watched.

Beck was hung up, gagged, choked and beaten continuously for four hours. Martial art kicks, a bamboo rod, oxygen tubing and a metal pole were among the weapons used on her.

The story only gets worse.

[These details are taken directly from court statements made by the detectives who investigated.]

The beating started in the bedroom, but when Beck "leaned" into the television, they moved her to another room because they were worried about the safety of the electronics.

Beck passed out a couple of times, but they thought she was "faking it."

One of the murderers paused long enough to take photos of Beck, her body battered and broken, hanging from the ceiling.

Why does this haunt me so much, even beyond the simple horror of human decency? Because I know that yearning to serve, to be willing to accept pain and even cruelty for the sake of another's pleasure.

I'm not really much of a masochist. I suffer in order to please my master, and I know what it is to just keep breathing, trying to endure. To simply hang on through the next blow, and the next, in the knowledge that it will finally end and I will be rewarded with a kiss, a smile, a tender embrace from the master who has never, in all these years, violated my trust.

What keeps tearing at my heart is that Shirley Beck got none of that. She hung there for four hours, just trying to endure. *Four hours*. There would be no tender caresses or aftercare when it was done. No one would tend her injuries with smiles. No one would say, "I am proud of you."

She gave her trust to the wrong people. Maybe she went looking for BDSM for all the wrong reasons, but that doesn't make what happened her to any less tragic. She still wanted to be a good submissive. She wanted to offer her body, heart and mind up in service to someone that valued her.

It breaks my heart.

Her murderers have admitted she asked them to stop. Did they mean she "asked," or do they really mean she begged? She must have. What words did she manage between choking sobs and muffled screams of pain?

For Shirley Beck, the suffering just went on and on. I can't even comprehend that level of pain, the rising panic when it occurred to her that this time they were not going to stop. In the last moments of consciousness, did she realize that, to these people, she was nothing? To die in that kind of anguish, with that sense of betrayal, might have been even worse than the pain.

When tragedy hits in our kinky community, it is almost always an accident born from ignorance, negligence or just blatant stupidity. People just didn't think. Or maybe they were being as careful as they could be, and fate just fucked them over with some accident no one could have seen coming. It happens, and many of us hope that someone will not be crucified just because the justice system and the vanilla world don't understand what it is we do.

But this was not negligence or ignorance; this was just brutality. This case is the every worst of what the world thinks we are, and what they believe we do. It doesn't matter that these people, while known to some of us, were not really a part of our community, and that their behaviors have crossed so far beyond the bounds of decency that we would hardly call them human beings, let alone practitioners of sane, rational and consensual BDSM.

For every person out there who is still carrying the burden of a secret longing, still struggling to figure out what those desires say about them, and what to do about them, this case is a staggering blow.

Yet I am not hoping that this will be forgotten, or knocked out of the news cycle by some new atrocity. People should hear about this. They need to know about this. Will it frighten some people away? Probably.

Maybe some people need to be frightened. If you want to be a submissive, you need to make damned sure you have your head on tight, and that you understand your reasons for being here, and if you ever think for even one moment that you really deserve to be treated like shit, YOU SHOULD NOT PLAY THESE GAMES. When red flags start flying, so should you.

But this case is not really about BDSM or kink. It's about criminal inhumanity trying to hide under the sheep's leather clothing, about the bastards who dare to drape their sins in our kinky flag.

Do they lie to themselves, really believing they are one of us? Or do they know that they perpetrate the worst perversion of all? They take the things we have worked so hard to understand about ourselves, all the lessons we have learned and taught, all the trust we have earned and given, and they grind every bit of it into the dirt. And then they piss on it.

When I first heard about this, I was sick at heart. Today, I'm angry. I hope these people are nailed to the wall, that they are punished in every way and to every extent the law allows.

But I just keep thinking about those last four hours of Shirley Beck's life.

Epilogue on Shirley Beck's Murder

Needless to say, this crime rocked the local community, and there has been a lot of debate — some of it good, some of it pointless and just plain stupid — about what might have prevented it. What complicates the issue is that none of our kinky community seemed to know the people involved very well. There are many people who exist in their own little fringe groups and, for whatever reason, don't interact with the rest of the community much or at all.

Which is one of the reasons I am always leery of those who refuse to have anything to do with the community. It's possible they have perfectly valid reasons to avoid the rest of us, but it's also possible they are hiding something. At the very least, it often means they simply don't play well with others.

What is known is that some of the assailants had been seen at a local munch at least a time or two, but if Shirley Beck was ever with them, no one remembers or is willing to admit it. She and at least one of the people who killed her did have a profile on FetLife.

News reports stated several neighbors had been concerned over Beck's situation for some time. She had frequently been seen with bruises to the face, and seemed very "skittish." One neighbor approached her just the day before her death, suggesting she go to a shelter, but Beck told him, "I'll be alright."

I've been following the news and searching online periodically, but have seen no follow-up to this case. It appears that this is just another blip on the radar, shocking people for a few days and then being forgotten.

I won't forget. I can't.

74323272R00104

Made in the USA
Columbia, SC
11 September 2019